ICE SKATING

Steps to Success

Karin Künzle-Watson
Professional Ice Skating Instructor
Coeur D'Alene, Idaho

Stephen J. DeArmond
Professor of Neuropathology and Neurology
University of California, San Francisco

Human Kinetics

Library of Congress Cataloging-in-Publication Data

Künzle-Watson, Karin, 1954-
Ice skating / Karin Künzle-Watson, Stephen J. DeArmond.
p. cm.
ISBN 0-87322-669-0 (trade paper)
1. Skating. I. DeArmond, Stephen J. II. Title.
GV849.K86 1996
796.91--dc20   95-31414
                                                  CIP

ISBN: 0-87322-669-0

Developmental Editor: Judy Patterson Wright, PhD
Assistant Editor: John Wentworth
Proofreader: Pam Johnson
Typesetter and Layout Artist: Kathy Boudreau-Fuoss
Text Designer: Keith Blomberg
Cover Designer: Jack Davis
Photographer (cover): Sharon Chester
Illustrators: Richard Becker, Stephen J. DeArmond, and Patricia R. Spilman
Photography for Illustrations: Richard Dawson
Printer: United Graphics

Instructional Designer for the Steps to Success Activity Series: Joan N. Vickers, EdD, University of Calgary, Calgary, Alberta, Canada

Human Kinetics books are available at special discounts for bulk purchase. Special editions or book excerpts can also be created to specification. For details, contact the Special Sales Manager at Human Kinetics.

Printed in the United States of America   10 9 8 7 6 5 4 3 2

Human Kinetics
P.O. Box 5076, Champaign, IL 61825-5076
1-800-747-4457

Canada: Human Kinetics, Box 24040, Windsor, ON N8Y 4Y9
1-800-465-7301 (in Canada only)

Europe: Human Kinetics, P.O. Box IW14, Leeds LS16 6TR, United Kingdom
(44) 1132 781708

Australia: Human Kinetics, 2 Ingrid Street, Clapham 5062, South Australia
(08) 371 3755

New Zealand: Human Kinetics, P.O. Box 105-231, Auckland 1
(09) 523 3462

Contents

PREFACE

This book describes and illustrates basic principles that are the foundation of all types and levels of ice skating. The steps to learn these principles successfully are presented as a series of exercises and skills that are, by and large, similar to the ISIA (Ice Skating Institute of America) and USFSA (United States Figure Skating Association) programs for beginning and intermediate skaters. These principles have evolved over the past 2 centuries, initially through trial and error. Over the past 50 years, 16-mm movies, video tapes, and computer analysis of elite skaters have further advanced our understanding. However, these principles are not presented in succinct detail in any contemporary book and may not be taught to the recreational ice skater. Adherence to these basic principles helps beginning skaters develop the balance and control necessary to skate safely and enables intermediate and advanced skaters to skate with power and style. In this book, we have deliberately concentrated on five fundamental principles rather than on more advanced skills such as jumps, spins, dance, or hockey.

Only a few ice skating instruction books are available today. These other books generally focus on the young, competitive, or professional skater and emphasize single, double, and triple jumps, spins, choreography, and artistic expression. These books provide only a brief overview of basic mechanisms and are not very helpful to the beginning or recreational skater. The authors of these books assume that the student will learn the basics through professional instruction. Unfortunately, not everyone has the opportunity to get good personal instruction. Although this book does not eliminate the need for lessons, it will help all skaters understand the basic maxims of ice skating. We hope to stimulate an awareness of body positioning that will lead to safe, enjoyable, and successful skating.

This book is unusual in that it was written by a teacher and her student. Karin Künzle-Watson began skating at the age of 5. Winner of many titles and competitions, Karin has also completed the equivalent of a university Masters thesis on ice skating. The theory of ice skating she presents here was developed from her teachers, her friendship and interaction with colleagues, and personal trial and error over 21 years of teaching ice skating. Her coauthor and student of several years, Stephen DeArmond, is a physician and medical school professor. Steve began recreational skating at the age of 47 because he wanted a high-energy, low-impact exercise enjoyable enough to do regularly three or four times a week. He chose freestyle skating for its challenge and its potential to improve and maintain strength and coordination. In Karin, Steve found a mentor who fully understood the mechanics and principles of ice skating and who had the patience and skill to teach them.

All of the instructional illustrations in the book feature Karin because her strong athletic style can be a model for both men and women. The illustrations at the front of each section demonstrate the wide range of outdoor locations for skating and celebrate the wide variety of people who enjoy ice skating today. Even if you don't live in a region with naturally frozen ponds, lakes, or outdoor rinks, you probably have access to indoor rinks. Some rinks are popular and well advertised; others are hidden away.

The authors would like to thank all who made this book possible. We owe our gratitude to the Winter Lodge ice skating rink in Palo Alto, California, for uninterrupted ice time, which allowed us to take the photographs of Karin that were the basis of the illustrative drawings. We also thank Sam Smith at the Winter Lodge for his help in preparing each photography session. Special thanks goes to Richard Dawson of Palo Alto for his sports photography expertise on numerous cold mornings at the rink. We are grateful to our two illustrators, Patricia Renaut Spilman of Mill Valley, who made the final illustrations of Karin, and Richard Becker of Redwood City, who completed all of the illustrations depicting outdoor rinks. Our thanks are also given to Al Fabrizio and R.J. Johns of Camera Graphics in Palo Alto for their advice and expertise in making the final camera-ready figures and to the Harlick ice skate boot company of San Carlos, California, for graciously supplying the ice skates used for the cover photo. Special thanks go to Bill and Lee Reynolds of Chadds Ford, Pennsylvania, and to Dr. Robert and Donna Hammil of Underhill, Vermont, for extending their homes and hospitality to Richard Becker and Steve DeArmond. Lee Reynolds and Donna Hammil were particularly generous with their time, guiding Richard and Steve to interesting and historical ice skating ponds and lakes. Thanks to the Human Kinetics staff, especially Ted Miller for his excitement about our project and Dr. Judy Patterson Wright for her patience and help in bringing this book to print. Finally, we most enthusiastically want to thank our spouses, not only for putting their lives on hold for 2 years, but also for the help they gave us. Jerry Watson helped with the layout, organization, and production of each stage of the book. Dr. Bernadette DeArmond helped edit the many drafts of the text.

THE STEPS TO SUCCESS STAIRCASE

Get ready to climb a staircase to ice skating success. Whether you want to skate because it's fun or because you want to compete in figure skating, ice dancing, or ice hockey, the concepts and basic skills you need to learn are described here in a sequence that allows you to pick them up at your own pace. Remember—you cannot leap to the top; you get there by climbing one step at a time.

Each of the 11 steps you will take is an easy and logical progression from the one before it. The first two steps provide a foundation—you'll learn correct posture, how to control your hips and shoulders, and how to best gain forward speed. In steps that follow, you'll learn methods of stopping and ways to gain and maintain forward and backward speed with both feet on the ice. We'll describe methods for turning up the power to gain maximal speed during forward stroking in a straight line and on a curve. As you reach the middle of the staircase, you'll learn the most popular two-foot methods to change direction from forward to backward without loss of control or speed, and we'll show you how to maintain and gain speed with backward power skating. Next, as you near the top of the staircase, the final two steps teach the skills you'll need to climb beyond this book to advanced skating maneuvers such as jumps, spins, footwork, and dance. You'll learn to command the edges of your skates, as they are the ultimate source of all power and control in ice skating.

Familiarize yourself with the Sport of Ice Skating and the Ice Skating Equipment sections to learn about ice skates and how to care for them, how to warm up and stretch for each skating session, how to cool down and stretch at the end of each session, how to protect yourself from skating injuries, and how to fall, recover, and get back up.

Follow this same sequence for each step as you climb the staircase to ice skating success:

1. Read the explanations of what is covered in the step, why the step is important, and how to perform or apply the step's focus, which may be an essential skill, concept, variation, or option.
2. Follow the Keys to Success illustrations showing exactly how to position your body to execute each basic skill successfully. When appropriate, we show you how to add style characteristics, smoothness, and consistency to the skill you are working on.
3. Study the Success Stoppers, which list common errors and recommendations for correcting them.
4. Practice the drills to help you improve your skills through repetition. Read the directions and the Success Goals for each drill. Then review the Success Checks and practice accordingly. You may choose to record your progress and compare it to the Success Goals for each drill.
5. As soon as you can attain all of the Success Goals for one step, you're ready for a qualified observer to evaluate your basic skill technique against the Keys to Success

checklists found in each step. Your observer should be an experienced skater who can help you assess your technique and tailor specific goals for you when they are needed.

6. Repeat these procedures for each of the 11 Steps to Success. Then review the Style and Efficiency section at the end of the book, which summarizes the most important ice skating skills in the form of questions to rate your progress.

Good luck on your step-by-step journey to learn the fundamental ice skating skills, build your confidence, and have fun!

Yosemite Park and Curry Company Ice Rink, Yosemite National Park, California.

THE SPORT OF ICE SKATING

Ice skating has been popular in Europe and Scandinavia as a mode of winter travel and enjoyment for over 1,000 years. Although ice skating was first restricted to latitudes and altitudes with prolonged cold temperatures, it is now enjoyed year-round in such unlikely places as Texas and Hong Kong. Whereas Olympic skaters in the first half of this century were generally from Northern Europe and Scandinavia, more recently champions have trained in indoor ice rinks around the world. Several successful new hockey franchises have sprung into existence in Florida, Texas, and California.

The popularity of ice skating in North America dates back to the earliest colonists. The degree of popularity in the United States 100 years ago is indicated by the half dozen or more ice skate manufacturers at the time. One of these, Barney and Berry of Springfield, Massachusetts, was producing 600,000 pairs of all-metal, clamp-on ice skates per year between 1865 and 1919. In the 1930s, the popularity of ice skating was greatly increased by films featuring Sonja Henie. Since then, TV broadcasters of Olympic, World, and National figure skating events and hockey have brought ice skating into the living rooms of people in all corners of the world. It is not surprising to see indoor and outdoor ice rinks crowded with ice dancers, hockey skaters, and freestyle skaters of all ages.

Young and old skate today for the same reasons they did in the past—because each facet of ice skating is fun. Many adults take up ice skating because regular exercise is necessary for well-being and deters the physical, mental, and behavioral ailments of advancing age. Ice skating is a particularly valuable activity because it strengthens muscles, improves balance, and provides important aerobic conditioning.

Evolution of the Ice Skate

Skates shaped from reindeer, elk, or horse bones or walrus teeth (tusks) fastened to leather footwear with straps have been used for hunting on the frozen fjords of Finland and Scandinavia for over 17 centuries (Figure 1). Wooden platform skates appeared in the 14th century (Figure 2). The earliest models had a wide flat bone or iron runner that ended under the heel for braking. This type of skate is shown in one of the earliest illustrations of ice skating, an AD 1443 woodcut depicting Saint Ludwina's ice skating accident in AD 1396. This skate is also shown in the 16th-century engraving of a Cornelius Dusart

Figure 1   Prehistoric bone ice skate discovered in Sweden.

■ **Figure 2** Wooden platform skate of the 14th century.

painting of a skater on flat Dutch skates propelling himself with a spiked staff (Figure 3). By the 18th century, runners became more blade-like. The traveling skate of North Holland of the late 1700s is an excellent example (Figure 4). Wooden platform skates that attached to shoes or boots by leather straps or metal clamps remained popular even into the 20th century. E.V. Bushnell invented the all-steel, clamp-on ice skate in Philadelphia, Pennsylvania, in 1848—a breakthrough in skating technology that led to the first spins and jumps.

■ **Figure 3** Sixteenth-century Dutch skater wearing wooden platform skates with flat runners and propelling himself with a spiked staff.

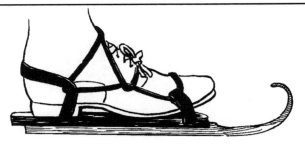

■ **Figure 4**   The wooden platform traveling skate with a narrow metal blade of North Holland in the late 1700s.

■ **Figure 5**   The Jackson Haines, two-stanchion, all-metal blade with heel and sole plates for boot attachment (circa 1865).

■ **Figure 6**   Haines' skate with addition of toepicks (rakes).

■ **Figure 7**   The closed-toe blade made from one piece of steel (1914).

The flamboyant American ice skater, Jackson Haines (1840-1875), emerged on the world ice skating scene at the time of the American Civil War and had a major impact on the evolution of ice skating. Haines broke away from the prevailing emphasis on tracing intricate patterns and emphasized uninhibited free skating that included spins, jumps, and dance movements. The Haines two-stanchion, all-metal blade with heel and sole plates to screw the blade to a boot (introduced around 1865; see Figure 5), was adopted quickly in most European countries. The addition of toepicks, or rakes (Figure 6), to the Haines skate made toepick jumps possible. John E. Strauss of St. Paul, Minnesota, a custom blade maker, made the final major improvement of the ice skate in 1914 with the first closed-toe blade from one piece of steel (Figure 7). This innovation lightened and strengthened the skate to give today's skater the freedom of the ice (Figure 8).

Figure 8 Innovations to the closed-toe blade have given today's skaters the freedom of the ice.

This figure was adapted from the book by Maribel Owen Vinson and is done in her memory. Her book, *The Fun of Figure Skating* (Harper and Row, New York, 1960), was one of the few to teach basic ice skating principles and to emphasize the pleasure of ice skating.

Preparing to Ice Skate

Before you venture onto the ice for the first time (or for the first time in years), you need to learn some basics to help you prepare. If you're a beginning ice skater, you'll want to read this section carefully, as we give information here on how to keep from hurting yourself on the ice. If you've already spent hours on the ice, you might just skim this section as review.

Warming Up and Cooling Down

Warm-up and cool-down exercises are essential to prevent injuries and to minimize muscle soreness and stiffness. They are important even if you'll only be skating for a short time. In time, as your skills progress, your warm-up will include a significant amount of skating. For now, be patient; know that even simple, off-ice warm-up exercises will benefit your skating—and your body will thank you!

Exercise physiologists generally agree about the sequence of warm-up and cool-down exercises that should accompany strenuous exercise. The sequence includes four parts:

1. The pre-exercise warm-up period prepares the body for strenuous skating by increasing deep body temperature, increasing blood flow to muscles, and elongating contracted ligaments and muscles. For ice skaters, such a warm-up usually takes the form of 5 to 10 minutes of forward and backward stroking around and across the rink at an easy,

comfortable pace. Beginning ice skaters should substitute stroking with off-ice jogging in place without skates for a few minutes.

2. The pre-exercise stretching period should follow the warm-up (because attempting to stretch "cold" muscles and tendons can cause injuries). The main reason to stretch is to increase the flexibility of leg and lower back muscles. Ice skaters usually stretch with ice skates on at the rink barrier or at a low wall on or off the ice. Several rules of stretching have been established by exercise physiologists, trainers, and athletes. The most important of these is that stretches should be done *gradually* without bouncing and with moderate intensity, because overstretching can cause pain and injury. A stretch should never cause pain. Stretches should be held for 10 to 20 seconds and without holding your breath.

3. After skating, a postexercise cool-down period of about 5 minutes is as important as the warm-up period. During the cool-down, continue skating but with decreased intensity (such as slow skating around the rink) to allow your heart rate and circulation to return to pre-exercise levels. Completely stopping activity suddenly after vigorous exercise can cause pooling of fluids and waste products in the lower extremities. These are believed to cause some of the soreness associated with exercising.

4. A postexercise stretching period follows the cool-down. It has been found that postexercise stretching greatly reduces muscle tension and soreness. For ice skaters, gentle exercises that stretch and strengthen your lower back muscles are most important. These stretches can be effective even if they are begun at home within an hour of the cool-down period.

The Weak-Ankles Myth

Many people avoid ice skating because of a fear of falling and a belief that they have "weak" ankles. This myth of weak ankles has probably been propagated by skaters using poor quality ice skates. In the absence of a serious medical condition, people don't have weak ankles—they simply have weak ice skates or have not fitted their skates properly. See the Equipment section for ways to assure a proper fit.

Falling and Getting Up

Falls will happen sooner or later—usually when you least expect them. They don't always hurt, as the same slipperiness that contributed to your fall will sometimes soften the blow. As a beginning skater, expect to fall, and don't be embarrassed. Even the best skaters fall now and then. In fact, it is when you get more confident and skate faster that the falls tend to come out of nowhere.

There are two categories of ice skating falls: those that could have been prevented (such as falls resulting from skating on cracked ice or from skating faster than your skills warrant), and the unavoidable falls (called *skating progress falls*) that occur while you're learning new and advanced skills. Even the number of unavoidable falls will decrease as you develop strength and as you master the basic ice skating principles presented in this book.

Beginning skaters most fear falling backward and striking their tail bones or the back of their heads. To minimize the risk of injury, try to land on the outer side of one of your thighs or on one side of your buttocks. Regardless of whether your fall is forward or backward, try to land on your side (see Figure 9). Falls taken at speed are usually far less painful than those that occur from a standing position. To avoid falls while standing still, stand with your feet at about a 45-degree angle until you can instinctively keep your weight over the balls of your feet.

Figure 9 Whether you fall backward or forward, try to land on the outer side of one of your thighs or on one side of your buttocks.

Figure 10 Get up from a fall from a kneeling position with both hands on the ice.

Falls rarely cause serious injuries. Several studies have found that the single most significant factor related to injuries is the skater's skill level. Most of those who get hurt have skated less than 10 times. Many of these injuries are preventable, as they are often related to unruly behavior, poor ice conditions, "showing off," and even alcohol abuse.

The safest way to get up from a fall (see Figure 10) is from a kneeling position with both hands on the ice. Place one foot flat on the ice between your hands. To stand, push your buttocks up and place your other foot close to the foot on the ice before straightening your legs.

Ice Skating Etiquette

Etiquette is usually related to safety—both your own and that of others. The following rules of etiquette on ice have changed little in the past century and are based on common sense:

- In most rinks, during public sessions when recreational skaters are on the ice, the general flow of traffic is counterclockwise on the perimeter of the rink. The center portion customarily is left to skaters practicing special skills.
- Follow the local rules, which sometimes include periods of skating clockwise. Common sense should tell you not to skate against the flow of traffic or practice stopping during a crowded session. Stops are considered special skills and can be practiced in the center of the rink.
- Even beginning skaters should be in enough control that they don't run into or grab onto fellow skaters.
- Get up quickly after a fall to prevent being an obstacle to other skaters and to avoid being run over.
- If you are capable, it is a nice gesture to assist someone who has fallen.
- Etiquette is mainly common sense and courtesy.

Skating pond and warming hut at Haverford College in Haverford, Pennsylvania.

ICE SKATING EQUIPMENT

Are you ready to learn to ice skate but not sure how to start? Here we'll introduce you to the three types of ice skates and their specialized uses. You'll learn the pros and cons of rental skates versus purchasing your own; what to look for in the construction of the skate and the way it should fit; how to lace your skates properly; and how to care for your boots and blades. You can review the various kinds of optional protective gear available and the reasons you might choose to use them.

Ice Skates and Their Care

When people talk about ice skates, they usually mean both boot and blade, though really only the blade is the skate. There are three kinds of skates: Figure skates, hockey skates, and speed skates (the dance skate is a variation of the figure skate), each designed to fulfill its unique function (see Figures 11a-c). Note that the speed skate blade is the narrowest,

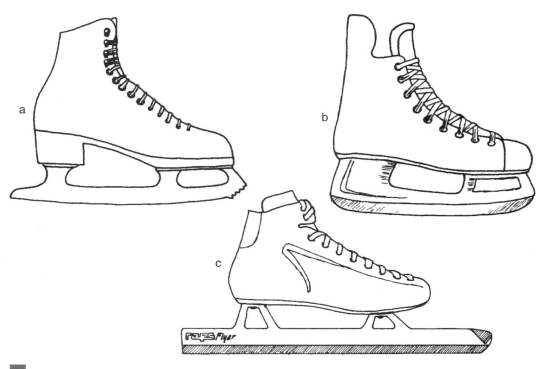

Figure 11 The three main types of ice skates and the cross-sectional profiles of their respective blades: (a) figure skate; (b) hockey skate; and (c) speed skate with an adjustable blade.

with a width of about 62/1,000 of an inch. The hockey skate is about 110/1,000 of an inch wide. The figure skate blade is the thickest, with a width of about 150/1,000 of an inch. The figure skate blade has the deepest groove between the edges of the blade (the *hollow*). The hollow's concave shape is created by a sharpening stone with a rounded grinding surface. The hollow of the hockey skate blade is less than that of figure blades, and the speed skate blade has no hollow. The hockey skate is constructed so that the boot is higher off the ice than either the speed or figure skate. This permits the ice hockey player to attain much steeper angles when cornering.

Figure Skates

Figure skates are the heaviest of the three types of skates because the boot, taller to cover more of the ankle, is constructed of heavy leather and the blade is more massive. To make it easier to slip your foot into the tall boot, lacing hooks (which make the laces easy to loosen) are used in the upper part of the boot. Comparing figure, hockey, and speed skates of equal quality, figure skates when laced properly will give you the best support. The most prominent feature of the figure skating blade is the *toepick*. The current design of the figure blade has evolved over hundreds of years. Its sturdiness, length, relative flatness, and its toepick give the most flexibility and possibilities on the ice.

While we particularly stress the use of figure skates because they are uniquely designed for the skills presented in this book, it is also possible to learn the skills on hockey skates. Doing so will be beneficial to those who plan to continue skating on them.

Hockey Skates

Hockey boots are usually made of a combination of leather and no-fray nylon weave. The boot ends shortly above the ankle with a higher piece in the back to protect the Achilles tendon. Unlike figure skates, hockey skates don't have hooks. They are tied with laces through eyelets. They will not give you as much support as a figure skate boot, but that's because no one expects hockey players to do jumps and spins. The sole of the hockey boot is made of plastic or fiberglass, and the blade is riveted to the sole. Compared to figure skate blades, hockey blades are shorter, narrower, and have a rounder rocker for very sharp turns. The biggest difference between hockey and figure blades, however, is the absence of toepicks in the hockey skate.

Speed Skates

Speed skates are completely different. Except for some selected principles and maneuvers presented early in this book, speed skates are not a good choice for the beginning or recreational skater. With speed skates, *weight* is the key word—every effort is made to keep them as light as possible. The boot is short with no ankle support and is made from a light supple leather. The blade is long with a straight edge instead of a rocker and is even thinner than hockey blades. For lightness, the blade is hollow on the top and made of lightweight steel. The left blade (when skating counterclockwise) on a pair of short-track speed skates is fastened toward the outside edge of the sole, whereas the blade on the right skate is fastened to the inside edge of the sole. New blade and fastening designs are available that allow the speed skater to move the position of the blade to adjust for short- and long-track skating. In general, speed skates are not recommended for beginners because the boot gives no support to the ankle and, because of the length and delicate construction of the blade, more balance and skill is required. Stopping and turning are difficult and are actually unwanted, as the kind of turning done on hockey and figure skates may bend or break the speed skate blade.

Rental Skates

Most rinks rent figure skates and hockey skates at a low cost. Until you are sure that you want to skate regularly, rental skates may do the job just fine. Unfortunately, because many people use the same rental skates and maintenance is not consistent, the quality of the edges and the firmness of the boots will vary.

Buying Your Own Skates

When you have decided that ice skating is for you, it's important to buy your own skates. Many people simply purchase the least expensive pair of skates available, such as from a department store or a catalog. If possible, it's better to spend a little more money and get higher quality equipment. With ice skates, you generally get what you pay for. Since you expect to do better on your own skates than on rentals (and rightly so), you may be disappointed if you try to skate on cheap equipment.

What to Look for in the Boot

The boot should be made of a high-quality leather firm enough to give your ankle support. The blade should be made of quality steel that will glide smoothly when sharpened correctly. Here are some tips:

■ Most new boots feel somewhat uncomfortable because the leather is stiff. Expect slight discomfort until the leather has had the chance to mold to the shape of your foot.

■ Boots should fit snugly. Better boots have padding around the ankles for comfort, and the tongues have a layer of sponge or lamb's wool. You want to be able to wiggle your toes, but when you bend your knees, your heel should stay on the bottom of the boot. Any movement of the heel within the boot is an invitation for blisters, sores, and even tendinitis.

■ Some of the snugness of a boot can be adjusted with the lacing, but if the boot squeezes your foot and pinches your toes, try a larger size or a different width.

■ Do not buy boots a size too big. Parents often think their kids will grow into them, which is true, but in the meantime, skating will be unnecessarily difficult. A second or third pair of socks is not a good solution. A part of successful skating is to feel the boot and have it fit snugly around the foot and ankle.

■ It's better to buy boots that fit and then, when your child outgrows them, trade them in at one of the skate exchanges sponsored by local skating clubs or rinks.

■ Take your time when you try on a pair of boots. Sometimes they feel fine for the first few minutes, but later they start hurting or feel too loose, and you wish you had chosen a different size. Don't be shy about asking for help with choosing the correct size.

■ The leather in a good pair of boots should not break down and become floppy after just a few sessions of skating. It should give you continuous support for a long time. As a beginner, you do not need the most expensive, custom-made boot, but comfort and support are of utmost importance. Without proper support, you'll have a hard time performing even the easiest moves. Without comfort, your concentration will be on fighting the pain, and the fun of skating will be lost.

Some of you with extremely sensitive feet may have a hard time even finding a pair of shoes for every day wear. If you fit this description, you really should consider buying custom-made boots. There are several reputable firms in the USA and Europe. Most skating professionals or skate shops can suggest a few.

What to Look for in the Blade

The beginning skater may be able to see little difference between an expensive and a low-cost blade. It can be very hard to distinguish the differences between superior and adequate steel. Often the size of the toepick will give you a clue. In general, the bigger the toepick, the more expensive the blade. Toepicks are used mostly for jumps. For a beginner, even small toepicks can be a nuisance, and large ones can be devastating.

Mounting the Blade

We recommend that you buy your boots and blades as separate units. It is always an advantage when the blades can be mounted onto the boots. Very few people stand perfectly straight on their feet, and proper blade mounting can adjust for such variables. Most rinks that sell boots and blades have staff who will mount your blades to your boots at no charge. In this case you don't have to worry about the mounting procedure.

Should you later want to change your beginner blades to a more advanced version, some of the holes for fastening the blade may not line up with the old holes in the sole of the boot. It is best to seal those holes with glue and wooden match sticks or toothpicks to keep moisture out of the sole of the boot. A couple of layers of lacquer, varnish, or clear nail polish will prevent water damage, and the screws that hold the blade to your boots will stay put a lot longer.

Proper Location of the Blade

On more expensive blades, some of the holes for fastening the blade to the boots are oval to allow the blade to slide in either direction. If you look carefully at the holes in these blades, you'll see that not all of them require the same kind of screws. The oval holes have straight sides and require flat-bottom screws, whereas the round holes are counter sunk and need screws to match.

Most skaters are more comfortable with their blades set slightly to the inside to make up for the natural tendency of ankles to pronate (bend inward). To learn whether your blades need to be set more to the inside or outside, look at your street shoes. If your sole is worn down on the outside of the shoe, place your blades slightly to the outside, as that is where your foot supports your weight and where you'll find your balance easiest. If the inside of the sole of the shoe is worn, move the blade to the inside. If the sole of your foot is particularly worn under the ball of the foot but the heel is worn on one side or the other, center the blade in the front but move it toward the worn side of the heel as needed to help find your balance. Often, just a small adjustment (a millimeter or two) is all that is required.

Sharpening Blades

All blades have to be sharpened. Usually the factory puts on the first grind to provide you with a blade that is skate ready. When your blades fail to grip the ice firmly and you start sliding sideways, it's past time to sharpen your blades. Don't wait until the blades are so dull that you skid and feel unstable. Maintaining a good edge is essential for progress.

A bad sharpening can ruin your blades. Getting your blade sharpened in hardware stores or at self-serve sharpening machines may be faster and cheaper, but this often leaves much to be desired. Ask a professional or a coach at the rink who they recommend in your area. Often you can find competent sharpeners at the rink. Proper grinding consists of sharpening the edges *and* readjusting the hollow that separates the edges. Too much hollow will cause the blades to cut too deeply in the ice, making them "stick" (feel slow and hard to maneuver). With too little hollow, you may still skid, lose your grip, and require a resharpening sooner.

Lacing Your Boots

Lacing your boots correctly is important for a proper fit and comfort. The lacing should be tightest around the ankle, where the support is needed most. You should not be able to slide a finger under the laces. Over the toes, keep the laces loose so you can wiggle your toes freely. Tighten the top of the boot to be comfortable.

Care of Boots

Caring for your skates prevents accidents and prolongs their life. Check the screws that fasten your blade to the boot regularly and tighten them when necessary. If they start turning without resistance, it's time to plug the hole (as described earlier) and reset the screw. Cracked lacquer and dark spots on your soles likely indicate moisture damage. In this case, apply another layer of lacquer. On the inside of your boots, perspiration, if not dried properly, will attract mold and eventually rot your boot from the inside out. It's best to take your skates out of the bag when you get home and give them a chance to dry thoroughly.

Skate guards protect the blades to avoid nicks, dings, and broken edges during the walk from the dressing room to the ice. You can buy skate guards at minimal cost at most rinks and sporting goods stores. Because they are made of rubber, the guards trap moisture and can cause rust, so don't leave them on the blade during storage. Instead, use cloth guards (made of terry cloth or any other heavy soft fabric) for storage. Cloth guards can also protect your blades from damage caused by banging together in the skate bag.

Protective Gear

On TV, you see the women in short skating dresses and the men in figure-hugging outfits—there's just no room there for protective gear. But don't forget that on TV you are seeing the end result of years of practice, so performance is usually at a very high level. Plus, part of the training of a competitive figure skater is to create the illusion that skating is easy. When you first start skating, your major concern should be safety—both your own and that of your fellow skaters. Any protective gear that makes you feel safer and gives you confidence is acceptable. When in-line roller skating became fashionable, knee pads, elbow pads, and wrist protectors were sold along with the roller blades as part of the equipment. Nowadays, many ice skaters also wear protective gear. Even a hat or a wool cap can protect you from a head injury.

As 70 percent of injuries among recreational and competitive ice skaters are to the wrist and hand (most result from falls to the ice or collisions with the rink barrier), we recommend that you wear thick gloves to protect your hands from a fall or from being run over by another skater. Wrist protectors, elbow pads, and knee pads are also recommended. Don't worry if you're surrounded by skaters who don't wear protective gear—you should never be embarrassed to be safe.

The Winter Lodge, community outdoor ice skating, Palo Alto, California.

STEP 1

PROPER SKATING POSTURE: DEVELOPING BALANCE

The secret of successful, dynamic, and safe ice skating is to center your body weight directly over the ice skate blade. Balance in turn depends on proper body alignment and carriage (posture). The way you feel varies from day to day and is often expressed in your body positions and posture and in the dynamics of your movements. Depending on how you feel, you may need to change your posture to skate. Ice skating will involve your entire body and virtually every muscle—maybe even some muscles you didn't know you had and would be happy to forget.

Our purpose in Step 1 is to increase your awareness of the optimal body posture for efficient, safe ice skating and to guide you through simple steps to achieve it. The maxims of ice skating posture, including the positions of your shoulders relative to your hips, have developed over the centuries. They evolved first by trial and error and more recently through study of movies and videotapes of accomplished skaters. You will learn what outstanding skaters do to make their skating fast, powerful, and seemingly effortless and what gives them the freedom to accomplish difficult and complex maneuvers.

Why Is Posture Important in Ice Skating?

The purpose of correct body posture is balance. Proper posture is uniquely important for ice skating because ice is slippery and ice skates are designed to take advantage of this slipperiness to glide forward and backward. Consequently, the distribution of your weight over the skates has a significant effect on how the skates, and you, will move. A slight forward or backward lean that's almost undetectable on a nonslippery surface can cause instability and even a fall on ice skates.

In addition to safety, proper posture is crucial for the balance you need to glide smoothly, stroke vigorously, and attain great speed. It allows you to execute quick and agile direction changes, perform expressive and creative footwork, express yourself to music, and eventually even to jump and spin. Correct posture allows you to focus muscular forces and the forces created by motion on the correct part of the blade. Finally, proper posture allows you to use your muscles most efficiently, reducing unwanted motions that cause loss of control and balance on the ice.

How to Execute the Proper Skating Posture

The basic skating posture has two components. The first centers your body weight over the front half of the skate blade. The second controls the position of your body weight from side to side and body rotation. These positions are so fundamental that we have designated them the first two principles of ice skating.

The first basic principle is to keep your body weight directly over the ball of your skating foot. The proper posture required to do this is first learned on two feet. Bend your knees, keep your chin up and your stomach tucked in, and, most important, keep the center of your chest bone (sternum) directly over an imaginary line interconnecting the toes of both feet. This places your weight over the front half of both blades (Figure 1.1a). A vertical line should fall from your sternum, past your knees, and between your toes (longer arrow), which places your body weight directly over the front half of the blades (shorter arrow). Arm and hand positions are also crucial for balance. Keep your hands at about waist to hip height, spread about 90 degrees apart, or so each hand is still visible out of the corners of your eyes. Your hands and arms should never pass behind your body, as that would pull your upper body backward and cause your shoulder blades to pass behind the vertical line to your heels. When this happens, your weight shifts to the back of your skate blades and causes unbalance.

The second principle of skating we call the "body box principle," a term we use to explain the relationship of hip and shoulder position. Keep the idea of the body box in mind whenever you're working on hip and shoulder placement. The four corners of the body box are the shoulders and the hips (Figure 1.1b). The shape of the box (i.e., whether it is tall or short, narrow or wide) is not important. What is important is that the hips and shoulders do not rotate or bend separately. Their relation to each other remains constant whether you're skating on one foot or two. Actually, there are two aspects of the hip and shoulder relation that must remain constant. First, your shoulders must remain parallel to your hips, like layers of a cake. Second, your hips

and shoulders must rotate equally and at the same time so that one never twists ahead of the other. The objective of the body box principle is to achieve stability by decreasing unneeded movements of the heavier body parts.

Up to now, we have discussed the basic skating posture on two feet. Now we move to one foot. The simplest way to experience the two components of basic body posture on one foot is to march in place. To facilitate transfer and placement of your full body weight over your skating foot (i.e., the foot on the ice), put your feet next to each other when you step. As you pick up one foot, bring your knee up and forward and try to keep the blade parallel to the ice (see Figure 1.1c). You only need a small, subtle shift of weight. If you keep your hips and shoulders parallel and not rotated in either direction, your arms low and in front with your hands in sight of peripheral vision, and your knees slightly bent, you limit the chances of losing control. Remember one of the basic laws of the physics of motion: For every action, there is an equal and opposite reaction. It is not unusual for a beginning skater to glide forward with just the first marching steps. The more pressure you apply to the blade of your skating foot before you lift it up, the more glide you'll get on the other foot.

FIGURE
1.1

KEYS TO SUCCESS

PROPER SKATING POSTURE

Principle #1:

Body Alignment
Over Skating Foot

1. Body weight over balls of feet ___
2. Sternum over toes ___
3. Knees bent ___
4. Arms extended forward at hip to waist level ___
5. Head upright ___

Principle #2:

Body Box

6. Shoulders parallel to ice ___
7. Hips parallel to ice ___
8. Hips and shoulders aligned ___

Proper Body Posture
During Weight Transfer

9. Maintain basic body posture ___
10. Keep feet close together ___
11. Alternately lift one foot off the ice ___

PROPER SKATING POSTURE SUCCESS STOPPERS

The two components of posture are critical to all aspects and types of ice skating because errors in posture become magnified when you stand, push, and glide on the ice. For example, proper forward gliding on skates requires that your body weight is directly over the skating blade or blades (first principle of skating). It is not like walking on pavement, where your weight can be distributed somewhere between your feet because the friction of your shoes on the pavement keeps your legs from spreading apart. If you step forward in a walking fashion on ice, your feet will slide apart. Very often, besides the distinct feeling of loss of balance, one of your toepicks can get caught in the ice. The latter is an invitation to a stumble (although it is a good way to get know your toepicks). Placing your body weight between your feet can also make it difficult to transfer weight from your back foot to your front foot.

Error	Correction
1. You fail to center your body weight over the front half of the skate blade (such as when your shoulder blades are behind the vertical line to your heels).	1. Place your sternum in line over your knees and toes.
2. You distort your body box by twisting your shoulders relative to your hips or by dipping your shoulders sideways.	2. Keep hips and shoulders in line, parallel to the ice and over your toes.
3. You bend your head forward and look down.	3. Keep your chin up to maintain proper skating posture. If you want to know what your skates are doing, look down once and memorize what they look like gliding on ice so you don't have to look down at them again!
4. You fail to bend your knees, which does not allow you to center your weight over the front third of the blades.	4. In virtually all sports, you control your balance by bending your knees to lower your center of gravity. Your hips and buttocks are moved slightly backward and counterbalance your chest, shoulders, and arms, which are moved slightly forward, resulting in a broader distribution of weight over your skating blade. Finally, when your knees are bent, you can adjust and shift the position of your body weight over your skating blade more easily and quickly.
5. Your feet are too far apart side to side and/or front to back.	5. Your feet tend to slide apart, and your body weight is between your feet rather than on top of them. Keep your feet close together.

DRILLS

1. Establish Balance Point

Beginning with the correct body posture, hold onto the rink barrier with one hand and slide your skate blades back and forth gently. Keep your weight in the center of your blades. Don't lean to the front or back. Even for advanced skaters, this principle stays the same—the weight remains directly over the skating foot or feet.

To get a feel of the dimensions and curvature of your blades, rock forward to your toepicks and then backward toward your heels.

 *Success Goal* = feeling a balanced stance ___

Success Check
- Body weight over balls of feet ___
- Head up ___

2. Transfer Weight From Skate to Skate

To feel weight transfer from skate to skate while maintaining proper posture, march in place. Proper skating posture includes gentle knee bend, weight directly over the blade, and the four corners of the body box aligned. Do this drill with or without holding onto the barrier.

 *Success Goal* = feeling a balanced weight transfer from skate to skate ___

Success Check
- Bend knees slightly ___
- Shoulders and hips parallel ___
- Weight over the blade ___

PROPER SKATING POSTURE SUCCESS SUMMARY

The two basic principles of ice skating posture presented in this step are very important, as they apply to virtually every maneuver you'll perform on skates. The more you fail to apply these principles while skating, the more you'll need to use therapeutic ice packs! Once you feel comfortable with the basic principles, determine whether you're executing the proper posture by asking your coach (or another trained observer) to rate your progress according to the checklists in Figure 1.1. For some, finding your balance and achieving proper posture will come automatically. For others, balancing on ice will be quite a challenge. Off the ice, check proper body alignment by observing your natural posture in front of a mirror. Any incidental misalignment of shoulder and hip relations will often become exaggerated during stressful situations such as learning how to ice skate. If your body box is straight and parallel, you're a good step closer to the correct posture. There is nothing at this stage that cannot be improved with practice.

Powder Mill Ice Skating Pond, Penfield Downs, Pennsylvania. Penfield Downs is a suburb of Philadelphia. Philadelphia was the site of the first U.S. ice skating club and it was there that the Bushnell all-steel clamp-on skate was invented in 1848, which is considered to be the breakthrough leading to spins and to the Lutz and triple Salchow jumps.

Figure adapted from a water color by Rose Ranieri Kirkpatrick, 1968.

STEP 2

PUSH AND GLIDE: MOVING AHEAD

Now that you can transfer weight from skate to skate by marching in place and you're comfortable with forward motion on the ice, you're ready to learn how to push to gain speed. You'll use the technique for forward pushing—also called *stroking*—repeatedly as you develop the skills presented in subsequent steps. There is no beginner or advanced push. The only difference is what the push will look like, and that will depend on several factors: your balance and speed, the force with which you extend the pushing leg, the degree of leg extension at the end of the push, the length of the glide between pushes, and your overall style. The more control you have of body posture, the better your push will look.

Here you'll learn the only effective push when one foot is on the ice: the inside edge push. Because only one foot is on the ice at once—either the gliding foot or the pushing foot—we say that this technique operates on the "light switch principle" (see Figure 2.1). We'll elaborate on this principle in later steps when it is applied to more advanced moves requiring sustained weight transfers.

Why Is the Inside Edge Push Important?

The inside edge push is the only way to get enough blade into the ice to exert maximum force with your legs. It's possible to push with toepicks on figure skates, but this works only at slow speeds and results in little speed gain. Hockey players and speed skaters do not even have toepicks on their blades. In skating, all pushes with only one foot on the ice are from an inside edge no matter if the movement after the push is forward or backward or to an inside or outside edge.

How to Execute the Inside Edge Push and Glide

The push is done on an inside edge from the portion of the blade under the ball of the foot (front one-half to one-third of the blade), *not* from the toepick. The front third of the blade stays in contact with the ice during the push. Generally, the pushing blade is at about a 45-degree angle to the gliding blade. Remember that the first principle of skating (presented in Step 1) involves keeping your body weight directly over your skating foot. Although the inside edge push *can* be made with both blades on the ice, it's far more efficient to have only one foot on the ice at once.

Unless you are gliding on two feet to reduce speed, your weight will always be on either your pushing blade (see Figure 2.1a) or your gliding blade (see Figure 2.1b), never both. You push with one foot, then glide on the other. At first, your glides may be very short, but when you start gliding faster you'll probably feel the urge to stroke faster, as well. This is a normal reaction. Keep in mind, however, that with every push you make, you accelerate, even if only slightly. If you get going too fast, the best way to slow down is to glide on two feet, keeping your feet close together. Avoid letting your feet drift apart, especially as you prepare for the next push.

As you complete a push, shift your weight to your gliding foot and lift your pushing foot off the ice; keep the raised blade parallel to the ice by bending your knee and lifting it forward. Now your weight is shifted to your gliding foot and you can either glide on two feet or prepare for your next push. Your gliding foot does not need to go straight forward. (In fact, it will probably go forward on an angle to the outside. With alternating pushes, this will create a zigzag pattern on the ice.) What's important is that your body box remains set and square to the tracing on the ice even while your weight is shifting from one skate to the other. Keep the center of your sternum over the toes of your gliding foot. A slight forward tilt of your body box will accomplish this.

Pushes are meant to produce speed. When you have enough speed, stop pushing and glide on one or two feet. Speed, as scary as it may be at first, can also be very exhilarating. Just feel the wind on your face!

FIGURE 2.1

KEYS TO SUCCESS

FORWARD INSIDE EDGE PUSH AND GLIDE

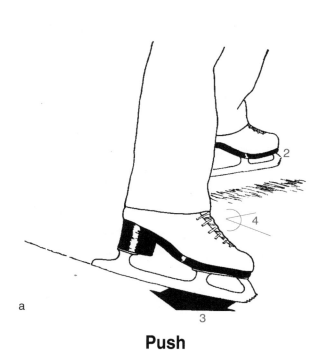

a

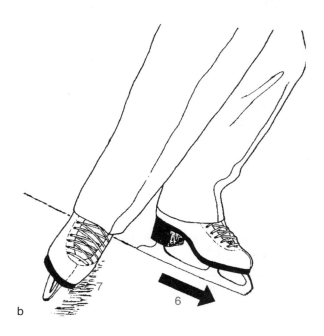

b

Push

1. Both knees bent ___
2. Lift one foot off the ice ___
3. Push from front third of inside edge of the blade on the ice ___
4. Angle the pushing blade about 45 degrees to the main skating direction___

Glide

5. Place gliding blade on the ice ___
6. Shift weight over ball of gliding foot ___
7. Simultaneously lift pushing foot off ice ___

FORWARD PUSH AND GLIDE SUCCESS STOPPERS

The push and glide technique is the same for beginners as it is for very advanced skaters. The potential to gain speed—a lot of speed if so desired—depends on how you execute the basic principles of body posture, alignment, and weight transfer. The better you avoid the following mistakes, the more effective your push and glide will be.

Error	Correction
1. Both feet remain on the ice when you push.	1. Maintain body weight over your gliding or pushing foot by keeping the center of your sternum over the toes of your foot on the ice. Shift weight with your feet close together.
2. You push with your toepick, lifting the heel of your pushing foot off the ice.	2. Push from the inside edge of the skate blade near the ball of your foot, then bend your knee by lifting it forward to return your pushing foot next to your skating foot.
3. You swing your arms gorilla style to try to gain speed, causing your upper body to swing in a countermotion to your hips, thus upsetting your body box.	3. Keep your arms at hip level, spread about 90 degrees apart and within vision.
4. You favor one foot in your pushing or gliding.	4. Practice transferring your weight from one skate to the other. If this does not come easily to you, all you can do is practice until it does.
5. You shift your weight too vigorously and upset your body box, leading to loss of control.	5. Keep your weight over your skating foot.
6. You lean backward when lifting a foot, which puts your weight on the back of the blade, increasing the chance of a fall.	6. Keep the center of your sternum over your toes.

FORWARD PUSH AND GLIDE

DRILLS

1. Alternate Push Drill

In proper skating posture, march in place. Begin pushing deliberately, using the forward part of the inside edge of either blade. Alternate pushing from one foot to the other.

Success goals will vary from individual to individual. Remember that a good way to glide forward without any effort is to glide on two feet. The more speed you gain, the longer the two-foot glide will be. For an effortless glide, use only the appropriate muscles that control skating posture and try to relax the other muscles. Beginning skaters often curl their toes to try to "hold onto the blade." This is almost a reflex action, but do try to keep your toes straight.

Success Goal =

a. 3 to 5 consecutive pushes under control ___
b. cruising around the rink with alternating pushes and longer and longer glides ___

To Increase Difficulty

• Do two or more consecutive pushes before gliding on two feet.

Success Check

• Push with forward part of inside edge of blade ___
• Alternate pushing from one foot to the other ___
• Glide on two feet ___

2. The Dip

So far, you have learned how to start moving from point A to point B. It is now time to learn your first trick. In the *dip* (see Figure 2.2), you bend your knees while keeping the relation of your shoulders to your hips constant through a major change in body position. In other words, changes occur only from your hips downward, keeping your body box alignment intact.

The dip starts after you gain speed and can glide on two feet. Stretch your arms out forward and then bend your knees to a crouch position with your abdomen touching your thighs. Keep your head and chest in front of your toes to counterbalance your rear end. Keep your feet close together with your knees straight over your toes. Your body weight should be supported equally by each foot.

This drill demands proper body position, as mistakes will be magnified. For example, if your weight is too far back on the blades and not over the balls of your feet, your skates will slide out from underneath you (with the obvious consequences). If you tend to lean forward, the dip will exaggerate this forward lean, which, if you're not bending your knees, will cause you to trip over your toepicks. In this case, although your nose might be in the right place, it's not really a dip if you don't bend your knees and lower your buttocks. An uneven distribution of weight to one of the blades will cause a curve, even with correct skating posture.

<u>Success Goal</u> = demonstrate proper body position by maintaining balance while gliding on two feet in the dip ___

Success Check

- Bend knees ___
- Lower buttocks toward the ice ___
- Keep body box alignment intact ___
- Balance body weight over feet ___

Figure 2.2   The dip demands proper body position.

FORWARD PUSH AND GLIDE SUCCESS SUMMARY

It's exciting to learn something as important as the push and glide this early on. Remember that there is no advanced version of a push or a glide. What you have learned in this step is the basis of your future on ice skates. Everything, including the most complex maneuvers, are derived from your ability to propel yourself in the desired direction while maintaining your balance. After practicing the drills, ask a trained observer to rate your progress using the checklist in Figure 2.1.

Gibson Pond, Great Falls, Montana. Named after the founder of the Great Falls Park System.

STEP 3

FORWARD STOPS: SLOWING DOWN

Learning to stop is important for your own safety as well as the safety of others. As you become a better, faster skater, you'll want to keep your stopping skills equal to your skating skills.

We'll discuss techniques for stopping while skating backward in Step 5, where backward skating is introduced. Here we'll focus on the three common methods of stopping while skating forward. The safest and easiest method is the *snowplow stop*. The *hockey stop* is used with higher speeds and is ideal in emergencies. The most attractive of the forward stops is the *T-stop*.

Why Learn How to Stop?

When beginners want to stop, they often rely on falling or crashing into other skaters or barriers at the edge of the rink. It is important to learn the proper ways to stop early because, as you learn to move faster, stopping is harder and takes more distance.

To practice stopping, find a location on the ice away from the main flow of skaters. Keep your distance from other skaters and be aware of them.

How to Do a Snowplow Stop

The snowplow stop is the safest and easiest method of reducing speed and stopping. Most instructors teach the two-foot method, which is similar to the snowplow stop used by skiers. In our experience, we

have found it is better to select one foot for stopping while the other remains gliding. Snow tends to be soft and can be pushed away by skis, whereas ice is hard and the edges of the ice skate blades are designed to cut into the ice rather than skid across it. To start, it is easier to skid one blade rather than two because you can vary the pressure on the skidding blade by shifting your weight between the gliding and skidding blades.

Start with some speed in a two-foot glide with both knees bent (see Figure 3.1a). Keep both feet on the ice but start shifting your weight to your gliding foot. Your other foot now becomes your "stopping foot." Keeping both knees bent, turn your stopping foot to a slight pigeon-toe position with the blade upright to avoid "grabbing" an edge. Your stopping foot will now begin to skid, and you will feel a great urge to straighten that leg. Don't! It's important to keep both knees bent throughout the stop. To add more pressure to your stopping foot, gradually transfer your body weight onto that foot. By the time you have come to a full stop, your stopping foot supports most of your body weight. To stop from more initial speed in a shorter distance, transfer your weight more rapidly. Try stopping with each foot before deciding which one works best for you.

To prevent curving to one side or the other while stopping, keep your body box facing the main direction of travel. Keep your hips and shoulders parallel to the ice (see Figure 3.1b).

FIGURE 3.1 **KEYS TO SUCCESS**

SNOWPLOW STOP
Preparation

1. Two-foot glide ___
2. Knees bent ___
3. Body box square to skating direction ___

Start of Skid and Slow Down

4. Turn in stopping foot (right) ___
5. Equal weight distribution ___

Weight Transfer and Stop

6. Increase weight on stopping foot ___
7. Keep knees bent ___
8. Body box remains square to skating direction ___

How to Do a Hockey Stop

The hockey stop is an ideal emergency stop because both feet are involved in the stopping process. Like the snowplow stop, deceleration is achieved by positioning the blade sideways to your skating direction. Start from a two-foot glide with bent knees, toes at the same level, and your body box facing the skating direction (see Figure 3.2a). Turn both feet sideways after a slight "bounce" to unweigh the skates (see Figure 3.2b). Keep your body box and arms facing forward and move them as little as possible. As you stop, your back foot carries a little more weight than your front foot and is on a slight outside edge, whereas your front foot is on an inside edge.

FIGURE
3.2 **KEYS TO SUCCESS**

HOCKEY STOP

Getting Ready to Stop

1. Two-foot glide ___
2. Knees bent ___
3. Body box square to line of travel ___
4. Hands visible at periphery of vision ___

Skidding to a Stop

5. Brief unweighing ___
6. Parallel turn of feet ___
7. Shoulders square to direction of travel ___
8. Minimize hip rotation ___
9. Increase knee bend with skid ___

How to Do a T-Stop

The T-stop is probably the best-looking stop, but it's also more difficult to master. Start with some speed on a two-foot glide to organize your body box and arms. Use one foot to continue the forward glide; lift your other foot and move it backward, with your knee and foot pointing 90 degrees away from the direction of travel (see Figure 3.3a). With the same knee bend and body box position, bring your stopping foot to the heel of your skating foot (Figure 3.3b). Note there

is a 90-degree angle between your skating foot and your stopping foot. Gently lower your stopping foot to the ice by keeping the blade upright. Avoid stepping on the heel of the gliding blade. As your body weight shifts onto the stopping blade, you'll slow down (Figure 3.3c). Keep your body box under control and facing in the skating direction. As you turn out your stopping leg and begin to stop, your body box will tend to rotate. To help prevent unwanted rotation of your body box, extend the arm of your stopping side to the front.

FIGURE 3.3 **KEYS TO SUCCESS**

T-STOP
Preparation

1. Two-foot glide ___
2. Organize body box ___
3. Hands at periphery of vision ___

Transfer Weight to Skating Foot

4. Lift stopping foot ___
5. Turn out stopping knee and foot (90 degrees) ___

Position Your Stopping Foot

6. Keep body box square to direction of travel ___
7. Bring stopping side arm (right) forward ___
8. Place stopping foot at heel of skating foot ___

Skid to a Stop

9. Shift weight to stopping foot slowly ___
10. Increase pressure on stopping foot to stop ___

FORWARD STOPS SUCCESS STOPPERS

All stops involve skidding on one or both blades. Since blades are designed mainly to go forward or backward, skidding requires a little more muscle control, particularly your abdominal and gluteus muscles. Firmness of these muscles helps prevent distortion of your body box and loss of control of your upper body, which can lurch forward or backward. Errors are sometimes compounded with higher speeds because of the greater forces required to turn and skid your blades while keeping your weight centered over your feet. When a stop begins with a glide on just one foot, such as the T-stop, it may create a new set of complexities and problems. For example, by lifting your stopping foot and placing it at the heel of your gliding foot, the chances of twisting your body box and stepping on the heel of your gliding blade are increased.

Error	Correction
1. Your knees are straight or stiff on stops.	1. Keep your knees bent to prevent your feet from sliding too far apart before you stop. This will also reduce the chances of tripping over the toepick. In the T-stop, both knees should be bent and open to a 90-degree angle.
2. Your stopping foot blade angles too much to the inside or outside edge.	2. Keep your stopping blade upright to produce a skid. For the snowplow stop, minimal pigeon-toeing helps. For the hockey stop, keeping the blades parallel and square to the skating direction helps. For the T-stop, turn the blade outward and lower the skate in an upright position onto the ice.
3. You rotate your body box, making it almost impossible to stop.	3. Organize your body box before you begin to stop. Keep your sternum forward, facing the line of travel. On the T-stop, bring the arm of your stopping foot side to the front.
4. You lean too far forward or too far backward.	4. Keep your body box square to the direction of travel. Keep your knees bent and the center of your sternum in line with your toes.

FORWARD STOPS

DRILLS

1. One-Foot Skid at the Barrier

This is obviously not a stop since you will be standing still and holding onto the barrier, but it will simulate the feeling of the blade skidding sideways on the ice rather than gliding. It will also give you a chance to learn the correct and most effective position of the blade for executing a snowplow stop. There are two parts to an effective blade position. First, the degree to which your stopping foot is pigeon-toed and second, the angle of the blade on the ice.

While standing sideways to the rink barrier and holding onto it with one hand, place one foot slightly ahead of the other and pigeon-toe it. Bend both knees. Transfer your weight from the supporting straight foot to the pigeon-toed foot while skidding it forward and to the side. Make your skid with the part of the blade beneath the ball of your foot. The more upright the blade, the easier it will be to skid it. An upright blade is achieved by knee bend and weight transfer to the skidding blade. Try your skid with the other foot to see which is most comfortable.

Success Goal = experiment to find your preferred foot to skid sideways on the ice ___

Success Check
• Make broad (versus narrow) skid marks on the ice ___
• Scrape snow-like particles off the surface of the ice ___

2. Snowplow Stop

For your very first snowplow stop, gain a little speed with a few strokes and get into a two-foot glide with your knees bent, your arms forward, and your body box aligned and facing the direction of travel. Stop! (Don't hold this position too long or you'll run out of speed before you can perform the stop.) Continue adding speed to develop confidence with this stop.

Success Goal = to come to a complete stop in a shorter distance than that necessary to attain speed ___

 **To Increase Difficulty**
• Test your ability to stop on an existing or imaginary line on the ice.
• Vary the speed before coming to a complete standstill.

Success Check
• Keep knees bent ___
• Transfer weight onto ball of stopping foot ___

3. Hockey Stop

To practice the hockey stop, do the same as for the snowplow stop but do a hockey stop instead. Usually, it is easier to do a hockey stop with more speed than is required for a snowplow stop. From a two-foot glide, unweigh your skates by slightly straightening your knees just prior to turning both feet sideways.

Success Goal = begin with the same speed as with a snowplow stop, but stop within a shorter distance ___

✔ **Success Check**

• Unweigh your skates prior to turning both feet sideways ___
• Keep toes at the same level ___
• Back foot carries more weight and is on a slight outside edge ___
• Front foot is on an inside edge ___
• Body box remains facing in the skating direction ___

To Increase Difficulty

• Increase speed.

To Decrease Difficulty

• Hold the barrier with one hand for support.

4. T-Stop

Take a few strokes to attain speed into a two-foot glide with your body box organized and perform the T-stop. Although we've included this stop along with the other forward stops, because it requires gliding on one blade and is mainly a stylish method of stopping, you may prefer to learn it later, after you're comfortable with one-foot gliding (which you'll learn in Step 4).

Success Goal = comfortably perform T-stops to both sides ___

✔ **Success Check**

• Bring instep of stopping foot to the heel of your skating foot ___
• Gently lower stopping foot to the ice ___
• Extend the arm of your stopping side to the front ___

To Increase Difficulty

• Vary the pressure on the skidding foot to learn how quickly you can come to a complete stop.

To Decrease Difficulty

• Only do the T-stop to one side.

FORWARD STOPS SUCCESS SUMMARY

For safety, keep your stopping skills equal to your other skating skills. It is not important which method of stopping you use as long as you can stop with control. Ask a trained partner, coach, or teacher to observe your execution of the three forward stops using the checklists in Figures 3.1, 3.2, and 3.3.

The Manhattan skyline towers over the Wollman Rink in Central Park, New York. Ice skating on ponds in Central Park has been the subject of illustrations and paintings for almost two centuries.

STEP 4

FORWARD SKATING MANEUVERS:
GAINING CONFIDENCE

Here we'll work on improving and expanding your skating ability to let you skate forward with increased speed and confidence. You'll begin with a series of two-foot gliding techniques including the *swizzle* and the *slalom* as alternate methods to gain speed and the *hockey glide*, which is a technique to achieve a controlled glide on a curve. You'll then progress to gliding on one foot over an extended distance.

These techniques are relatively simple, but as you'll be using them for as long as you skate, it's best to learn them well now. As your skating horizon expands, you'll probably want to take stylistic liberties with these simple maneuvers, which will change them drastically. For now, we'll focus on the basics.

Why Are Forward Maneuvers Important?

For the beginner, two-foot skating techniques are a safe and fun way to improve skills and move across the ice. Because these are performed on two feet, they may be more attractive to skaters still struggling with their balance. *Swizzles* will move you in a straight line, giving you the experience of gliding on edges for the first time. Unlike the swizzle, in which you skate in a straight line with both feet on an inside edge, the *slalom* introduces you to skating on curves and using both inside and outside edges. The slalom can be a very satisfying maneuver because it is an effortless way to gain speed and its rhythm, either fast or slow, can be adapted to music. The slalom results in consecutive alternating, relatively flat curves with both feet parallel and next to each other. The hockey glide also results in a curve, but it is in one direction with one foot in front of the other. The advantage of the hockey glide is that you can achieve very tight turns,

including U-turns, with a fair amount of speed. It is called a "hockey glide" because it's used frequently by hockey players. Except for hockey, all other forms of ice skating such as figure, freestyle, dance, and speed skating are done primarily on one foot. Power, efficiency, and style on ice skates all derive from balance on one blade. For this reason, we end this step by introducing you to extended one-foot gliding.

How to Execute a Swizzle

This is the first time you will experience an intentional glide on an inside edge of the blade. The maneuver is done entirely on an inside edge by placing your feet next to each other with a slight knee bend and equal body weight distribution (see Figure 4.1a). It is easier to do with a little speed at the start but it can also be done from a standstill. In either case, the goal is to maintain speed and eventually to gain speed. Starting from a two-foot glide, let your feet drift apart on an inside edge by steadily increasing your knee bend (see Figure 4.1b). When your feet are about hip- to shoulder-width apart, begin to rise out of the knee bend and turn your toes inward and forward while squeezing them back together (see Figure 4.1c). This will bring you back to the starting position. The swizzle should be long and slim in shape. While this is the most efficient method of gaining speed with the swizzle, deviating your feet wider than your shoulders can create some flare and make the swizzle more dynamic and fun. The weight stays evenly distributed with both feet tracing mirror patterns. Your body box remains square to your skating direction. Your arms are held waist high. Your hands remain in sight of the periphery of your vision.

FIGURE
4.1
KEYS TO SUCCESS

THE SWIZZLE

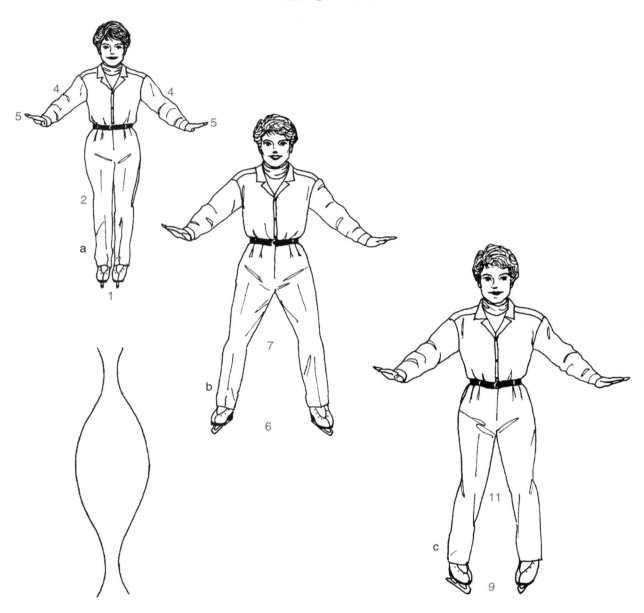

Pre-Swizzle

1. Feet together and parallel ___
2. Knees slightly bent ___
3. Body box square to direction of travel ___
4. Arms waist high ___
5. Hands at periphery of vision ___

Separation

6. Move feet apart ___
7. Increase knee bend ___
8. Body box remains unchanged ___

Return

9. Turn feet to inside ___
10. Squeeze feet together ___
11. Rise, but not completely, from knee bend ___
12. Bring feet back together, touching ___
13. Repeat maneuver ___

How to Execute the Slalom

The slalom shares similarities to downhill skiing. Your body box remains facing the main direction of travel with your knees directing your skates from side to side. Like the swizzle, the power for this forward movement with alternating curves comes from bending your knees. Both feet stay on the ice approximately one foot apart throughout (see Figure 4.2). Your weight shifts from one side to the other by bending the leg on the inside of the curve slightly more than the outside leg. The bent inside leg, which is supporting most of your body weight, skates on an outside edge (see Figures 4.2b and d). The skate on the outside of the circle is on an inside edge. At the beginning of a curve, your body is directly upright, your body box faces the main direction of travel, and your feet and knees are directed away from the main line of travel (see Figure 4.2a and c). As you bend your knees, your body leans to the inside of the curve with your shoulders and hips remaining parallel and your body box facing forward. As you curve back to the main line of travel, straighten your inside knee so that an equal amount of bend is present in both legs and your body is now directly upright again. As you begin the next and opposite curve, create a lean in the other direction by bending the new inside knee more than the new outside knee. Try to keep your head and your body box at a constant level above the ice and let your legs swing side to side underneath you with a pendular motion. Keep your arms out to the side at about a 90-degree angle to each other.

How to Execute the Hockey Glide

Although you'll eventually do hockey glides and turns with full speed, at this stage you might want to begin with a few pushes and a two-foot glide. Decide which direction you wish to turn. The direction of the curve will actually be determined by the inside edge of your back foot. For example, to do a left (counterclockwise) turn, move your left foot forward on an outside edge (see Figure 4.3a). As your left foot shifts forward, bend your right knee and place most of your body weight on your right foot. The turn will be steered by the inside edge of your right foot. In the final position, your thighs and knees are held tightly together to bring both feet in-line on the same circle. Your forward leg is straight, and your back leg is bent at the knee. To insure that your weight is mostly on your back foot, in addition to bending your back knee, keep your chest in line over the toes of your back foot (see Figure 4.3b). As your speed increases and you want to make tighter curves, your front leg will also need to be bent slightly.

In several of the upcoming steps, you will learn methods of turning which require rotation of your body box towards the center of the turn. This is not necessary for the hockey glide or the slalom. With the hockey glide, a lean to the center of the curve will occur automatically and its degree will be dependent on the speed and the tightness of the curve. Your body box should not be distorted as you lean. Do not drop your shoulder. Keep the distance between your shoulders and hips the same on both sides of your body.

FIGURE
4.2 **KEYS TO SUCCESS**

THE SLALOM

Preparation

1. Gain speed wtih basic skating pushes ___
2. Two-foot glide ___
3. Organize your body box ___

Initial Curve

4. Bend both knees ___
5. Turn knees and feet to one side ___
6. Hands at edge of peripheral vision ___

Transition Stage

7. Increase knee bend ___
8. Body box square to main direction of travel ___

Opposite Curve

9. Direct knees and feet to opposite direction ___

FIGURE
4.3

KEYS TO SUCCESS

THE HOCKEY GLIDE (TURN)

Preparation

1. Gain speed with basic skating pushes ___
2. Two-foot glide ___
3. Organize your body box ___

Execution

4. Slide inside foot forward (inside relative to the curve to be skated) ___
5. Shift weight to back foot (sternum over back foot) ___
6. Bend back knee ___
7. Press on inside edge of back blade ___

How to Execute the Forward One-Foot Glide

Start off with sufficient speed to carry you through the entire maneuver. The combination of speed and your arm position will help you to maintain balance. Your arms should be forward with hands between hip and waist level and at the edge of your peripheral vision. Begin with a two-foot glide, squeeze your buttocks together and tighten your abdominal muscles. Now lift a foot with knee pointing forward and blade parallel to the ice. As always, your weight has to be over your skating foot. In order to maintain the glide over an extended distance, you have to slightly tilt your body box onto a corner by lifting the free-leg side to bring the center of your sternum on a line directly over your toes. Balance is aided by keeping your free foot close to your skating ankle (see Figure 4.4). Note that your body box is not distorted even though it is tilted. Your shoulders and hips are parallel to each other.

FIGURE 4.4 **KEYS TO SUCCESS**

FORWARD ONE-FOOT GLIDE
Preparation

1. Gain speed with basic skating pushes ___
2. Two-foot glide ___
3. Organize your body box ___

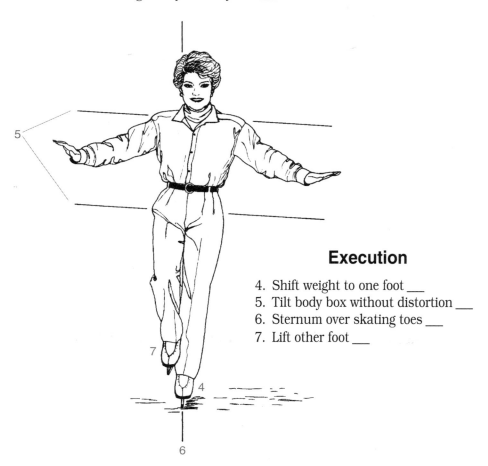

Execution

4. Shift weight to one foot ___
5. Tilt body box without distortion ___
6. Sternum over skating toes ___
7. Lift other foot ___

FORWARD SKATING MANEUVERS SUCCESS STOPPERS

Distortion and rotation of your body box and stiff knees are errors which can occur in all four of the maneuvers of this step. However, the causes of each of these errors and their results vary greatly among the maneuvers and require different corrections.

Error	Correction
Forward Swizzles	
1. Stiff knees.	1. This will shift your weight forward and may cause tripping over the toepicks especially when your feet are brought back together. Therefore, keep your knees bent and weight over the balls of your feet.
2. Uneven pattern.	2. This is usually the result of uneven weight distribution. Carry an equal amount of weight on each foot.
3. Rocking of your body box forward and backward.	3. Backward and forward motion of your upper body causes instability. Your shoulder blades should never pass the vertical line from the heel of your foot. If they do, a backward fall may occur.
4. Twisting or rotating your body box.	4. Keep your body box square to the direction of travel.
5. The angle of the skates is too steep.	5. The pattern of the swizzle should be long and slim. If the pattern gets too short, you usually skid like a snowplow stop and, instead of getting speed, you slow down.
6. Not enough inside edge (skates too upright).	6. Be sure your skates are on inside edges.
Slalom	
1. Not enough knee bend.	1. Your knees should always be bent. Your knee bend is deepest at the furthest point along the arc of the curve and least at the transition from one arc to the other. The speed gained is directly related to the depth of the knee bends which generate the power.
2. Rotating your body box.	2. This is usually associated with arm swinging. This makes the transition from one arc to the other difficult to complete. Rotating your body box and swinging your arms is very inefficient because it takes a tremendous amount of energy to correct for their rotation.
3. Picking up a foot and pushing with its toepick.	3. Speed is gained through knee bend, weight shift, and edges on both skates and not by pushes with a single foot.

Error	Correction
Hockey Glide	
1. Feet side by side rather than in line.	1. This is the most common error with the hockey glide and results in a flat curve, not the tight curve that is the hallmark of a hockey glide. One of the reasons you may have difficulties getting your feet in line is that too much weight has been placed on your forward foot and on its outside edge. The correction is to shift the majority of your weight to your back foot.
2. Insufficient knee bend in your back leg.	2. This will result in your weight being distributed between your feet instead of mostly on your back foot. Your front foot should only support the weight of your front leg. Most of your body weight must be on your back foot whose inside edge will determine how tight the curve will be. With both feet on the ice in an in-line position, the only way to get most of your weight on your back foot is to bend your back knee.
3. Leaning and rotating your body box to the outside of the curve being skated.	3. This is another common mistake. This causes your body to lean to the wrong direction and to "fall out of the curve." Lean, without distortion of your body box, should be to the inside of the curve.
One-Foot Glide	
1. The most dangerous error is to lean backwards when one foot is picked up.	1. Keep the center of your sternum directly over the toes of your skating foot.
2. The most common error is not shifting your weight to your skating foot.	2. Consciously shift the center of your sternum over the toes of your skating foot and keep the lifted free leg close to your skating leg.
3. Not uncommonly, beginning skaters twist and distort their body box by counterrotating their arms when the foot is picked up.	3. Keep your arms as stationary as possible with your hands in view of your peripheral vision.
4. Picking up your free leg from your heel, which places your foot behind and away from the skating axis.	4. Lift your foot off the ice by raising your knee upward keeping your lifted blade parallel to the ice.

FORWARD SKATING MANEUVERS

DRILLS

1. Swizzles From a Glide

Start the swizzles from a two-foot glide. Bend your knees more and let your feet drift shoulder-width apart, keeping equal body weight on the inside edges. To come back to your starting position, rise out of your knee bend and turn your toes inward, squeezing them back together again.

Success Goal = maintain speed while doing the swizzles ___

Success Check
- Make a long, slim, hourglass shape on the ice ___
- Alternately press toes apart, then toes inward ___
- Use inside edges ___

To Increase Difficulty
- Gain speed while doing the swizzles.

To Decrease Difficulty
- Let your feet drift only 4 to 6 inches apart.

2. Swizzles From a Standstill

To determine whether you can gain speed and not just maintain speed you gained with pushes, as may have been the case with Drill 1, begin the swizzles from a standstill. To judge your success, do a set number of swizzles, such as three or four, and come to a complete stop with a snowplow stop. Observe the distance covered on the ice. Repeat.

Success Goal = to traverse as great a distance as possible and to stop in the shortest possible distance ___

Success Check
- Body box remains square to the skating direction ___
- Arms are held hip high ___

3. Slalom With Obstacles

If cones or similar obstacles are available and can be used at your rink, set them at equal intervals on the ice. Skate through this slalom course at different speeds. Keep your head and body box at a constant level. Let your legs swing side to side underneath you with a pendular motion. Keep your arms out to the side for balance.

Success Goal = to skate symmetrical and equal size curves to both sides ___

Success Check
- Both feet stay on the ice ___
- Weight shifts from one side to the other ___

To Increase Difficulty
- Shorten the distance between the obstacles.

To Decrease Difficulty
- Lengthen the distance between the obstacles.

4. Freestyle Slalom

Vary the size of the arcs and the rate at which you change direction. Music is very useful to gain the rhythm needed for this maneuver. This exercise can be used to interpret music.

Success Goal = to create a rhythmic pattern ___

Success Check
- Shoulders and hips remain parallel ___
- Body box square to direction of travel ___

To Increase Difficulty
- Make curves asymmetrical.

To Decrease Difficulty
- Keep curves symmetrical.

5. Hockey Glide

Start with a few pushes into a two-foot glide. With varying amounts of speed, attempt hockey glides to both sides. The direction of the curve is determined by the inside edge of your back foot. Let one foot shift forward, and bend your back knee to hold most of your body weight. Maintain this forward-backward stride position during the curve. Repeat to the opposite side.

Success Goal = to make a curve with one foot in front of the other to both sides ___

Success Check
- Front foot is on an outside edge ___
- Back foot is on an inside edge ___

To Increase Difficulty
- Make a complete U-turn.
- Increase hockey glide speed.
- Make tighter curves.

To Decrease Difficulty
- Make shallow curves.

6. Forward One-Foot Glide

Use pushes to gain speed into a two-foot glide. Then, let your body weight shift onto one foot and continue your glide. Attempt the one-foot glide to both sides and at varying speeds. Hold each as long as possible. Like riding a bicycle, speed aids balance. Unfamiliarity of skating on one foot may cause you to feel the urge to put the second foot on the ice after a very short lift. This may not be a technical problem but just a lack of confidence. With time and practice, that urge will disappear.

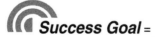

Success Goal =
a. to glide the entire width of the ice rink ___
b. to glide the entire length of the ice rink ___

Success Check
- Keep your free foot close to the skating ankle ___
- Bring arms forward slightly for balance ___
- Keep shoulders and hips parallel ___

FORWARD SKATING MANEUVERS SUCCESS SUMMARY

In the first three steps you learned the basic posture, how to push and move forward, and how to stop. In this step, you have improved your ability to make single and consecutive curves and to glide on one foot. The ease with which you can perform these maneuvers will ultimately determine your comfort level with more complex moves in the future. The exercises in this step really give you a great opportunity to find out how important the basic ice skating posture is with its emphasis on control of the body box and maintenance of weight over the skating foot. Hopefully you made some mistakes with posture while learning these maneuvers because they may have taught you how important they are for control and how disruptive and energy consuming they can be. An informed observer can help you rate your progress with swizzles, slaloms, hockey glides, and one-foot glides to this point according to the checklists in Figures 4.1 through 4.4.

Twin Lakes, Greenville, Delaware, has been used for ice skating as far back as the eighteenth century.

STEP 5

BACKWARD SKATING AND STOPPING: DOUBLING YOUR OPTIONS

Two major benefits of backward skating are that you can generate speed with less effort than forward skating and you don't have to worry about your toepicks. On the negative side, skating backward can be scary for some beginners. This fear often results from lack of confidence and not being able to see where you are going. In this step, we'll start with a very simple method to get the feeling of gliding backward: pushing off a wall. We'll then progress to two-foot techniques for generating and maintaining backward speed: *swizzles* and *wiggles*. You'll also learn a simple and effective method for backward stopping. The step finishes with backward one-foot glides and stroking, moves that are quite challenging.

Why Is Backward Skating Important?

Speed skaters virtually never skate backward on purpose, and they seem to be quite happy! So why *is* backward skating important? Because it doubles the options and pleasure of all other types of ice skating. For every maneuver you can perform forward, there is a backward counterpart. Backward skating is essential for defense in hockey. Ice dancing could not exist without backward skating, as at least one partner is skating backward in many dance sequences. Much of the excitement in figure skating that results from turning, footwork, spinning, and jumping would not be possible without backward skating. Although some of the beginning maneuvers have funny names and appear to be so basic that they are only used as a mechanism to become comfortable with backward

skating, you'll be amazed how handy these are and how often even the most advanced skaters use them.

Since you can attain as much, or even greater, speed skating backward as forward, you must learn how to stop as well when you're going backward as when you're going forward. The one-sided backward snowplow stop is an efficient and easy way to stop at all speeds, whereas stopping by scratching with your toepick, analogous to roller skating stops, is *not* a good solution on the ice. Besides damaging the ice, such stops only work at slow speeds. Hockey skaters don't have this option, as hockey blades don't have toepicks; yet hockey players can stop instantly from very high speeds.

How to Execute Your First Backward Glide (Push Off Wall)

Assuming that you can't gain speed skating backward yet, the best way to get a feeling of gliding backward is to push backward off a wall (see Figure 5.1). Begin by facing the rink barrier. Place your hands on the barrier with your elbows bent, but don't lean on the wall. Your feet should be close together and parallel supporting your body weight equally. To prevent your upper body from swaying too far backward or too far forward when you push off, keep the center of your sternum over your toes and tighten your abdominal muscles. Now push away from the barrier. The harder you push, the faster and longer your glide will be.

FIGURE
5.1
KEYS TO SUCCESS

PUSH OFF WALL

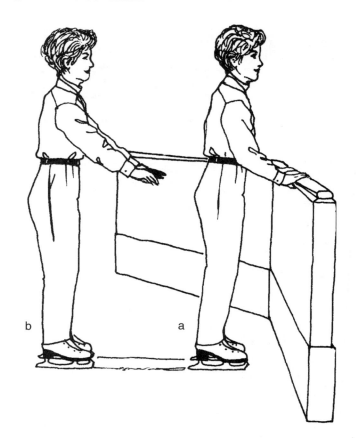

Prepare to Push Off Wall

1. Face rink barrier __
2. Place feet close together and parallel __
3. Distribute weight equally __
4. Hands on barrier with bent arms __

The First Backward Glide

5. Push off wall __
6. Maintain basic skating posture __
   • body box (shoulders and hips aligned) __
   • weight over skates __
7. Keep feet close and parallel __

How to Execute the Backward Swizzle

This is the backward equivalent of the forward swizzle and, like the forward swizzle, you use it to gain speed. It is probably best to start from a two-foot glide, such as a push from the barrier. Both feet support an equal amount of weight, but this time you want to be on the inside edges. Slowly, force your heels apart to about the width of your hips, and then gradually bring your heels back together (see Figure 5.2). If you recall, in the forward swizzle your toes pointed in the direction of skating. Here, your heels determine the direction, so they are the first to point out or in. Like the forward swizzle, your backward swizzle should be long and slender. A slight pigeon-toed position and a good knee bend allow you to gain speed as your skates move to the "fat" part of the swizzle. As you bring your feet together, rise out of your knee bend to come back to your original starting position. Repeat this process. During this entire maneuver, your body box remains square to your skating direction, and your arms are extended with your hands at the edge of your peripheral vision and at hip to waist level.

FIGURE 5.2 KEYS TO SUCCESS

THE BACKWARD SWIZZLE

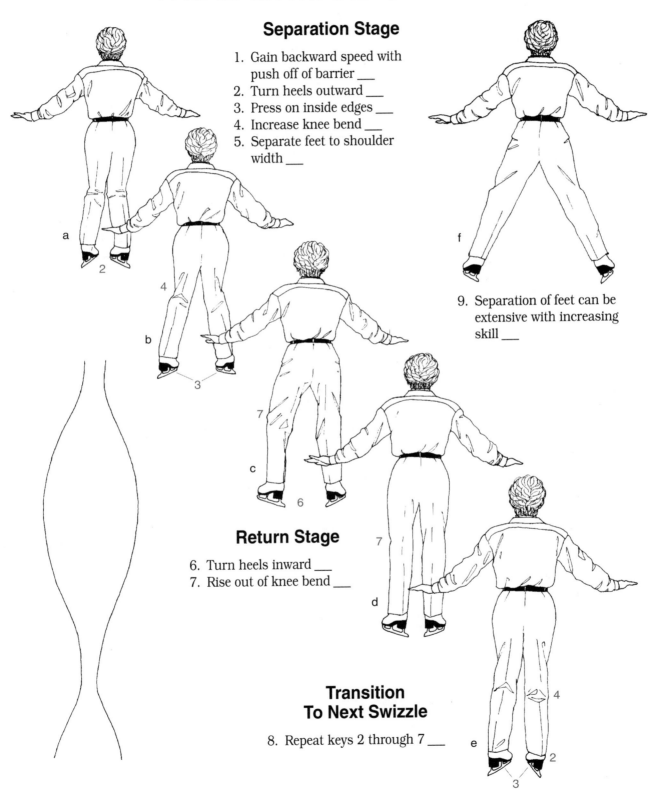

Separation Stage

1. Gain backward speed with push off of barrier ___
2. Turn heels outward ___
3. Press on inside edges ___
4. Increase knee bend ___
5. Separate feet to shoulder width ___

9. Separation of feet can be extensive with increasing skill ___

Return Stage

6. Turn heels inward ___
7. Rise out of knee bend ___

Transition To Next Swizzle

8. Repeat keys 2 through 7 ___

How to Execute the Backward Wiggle

The backward wiggle is comparable to the forward slalom and can be used to gain relatively fast, controlled speeds. It is a favorite method of hockey players, who use it to skate backward particularly on defense. You maintain control and stability because both blades remain on the ice. You gain speed by transferring your weight from one side to the other, *not* by wiggling your hips hula style. This weight transfer is done by bending the leg on the inside of the curve slightly more than the other leg (see Figure 5.3). The leg with more bend, which supports most of your body weight, is on an outside edge. The hips and shoulders remain square to the main direction of travel rather than turning along with your heels. All movement should be from your knees down, with your heels turning alternately outward in one direction and then in the other to produce the appropriate slalom-like pattern on the ice.

How to Execute the Backward Teeter-Totter Push

As with forward skating, the key to backward skating is to transfer body weight completely onto one skating foot. For the beginning student just developing the confidence to glide on one blade, the backward teeter-totter exercise is a simple way to experience lifting one foot off the ice and transferring weight completely to the other while moving backward. The teeter-totter is a preparation for backward stroking (as marching in place was a preparation for forward pushing and gliding). Like any movement in skating, distance is gained by gliding rather than stepping.

Backward teeter-totters begin from either a standstill or a backward two-foot glide. From a stand-still position, stand pigeon-toed with your big toes almost touching (see Figure 5.4a). Pick up one foot by lifting your knee upward and forward. Keep your lifted foot in the pigeon-toed position with the blade parallel to the ice. As you lift one foot, your weight transfers naturally to the other foot. Your body box tilts slightly in that direction to effectively transfer the weight of your body directly over your skating foot, which is necessary for balance. When done correctly, a straight line perpendicular to the surface of the ice will pass from your skating foot through your opposite shoulder (see Figure 5.4b).

Just lifting one foot from a standstill does not create any backward movement. As with all one-foot pushes, the backward push is done from the inside edge of the foot that supports your weight and is on the ice. The more pressure you apply to the inside edge of your pushing foot at the moment of weight transfer to the gliding foot, the more speed you'll gain. With increased speed, your glides will become longer, and the patterns may expand. The pattern on the ice looks like a zigzag rather than consecutive half-circle curves. As you lift your free leg with each push, keep your free foot pigeon-toed, parallel to the ice, and in front and close to your skating leg. Throughout, your body box remains square to your main direction of travel (not along each zigzag leg), and your arms are at hip level with hands in sight of your peripheral vision.

How to Execute the Backward One-Foot Glide

Once you can shift your weight to one foot for short distances with teeter-totter pushes, it's time to learn to glide backward for extended distances. Extended backward one-foot glides take a lot of balance and are easier to do if you've gained speed from backward wiggles, swizzles, or teeter-totter pushes.

Before starting, organize your body box and set your basic posture with a backward two-foot glide. To initiate a one-foot glide, your body weight needs to shift over your skating foot by tilting your body box slightly. This lifts your free side, causing the skating axis to pass from your skating foot through your skating leg to your free (opposite) shoulder (see Figure 5.5). With a sustained one-foot glide, your feet are parallel and your skating leg is straight but not hyperextended. Pick up one foot by bending and lifting your knee forward so that the blade stays parallel to the ice with your free foot next to your skating leg. As you pick up your foot, tighten your abdominal and buttocks muscles. Extend your arms, with your hands at hip to waist level and at the edge of your vision.

FIGURE
5.3

KEYS TO SUCCESS

BACKWARD WIGGLES

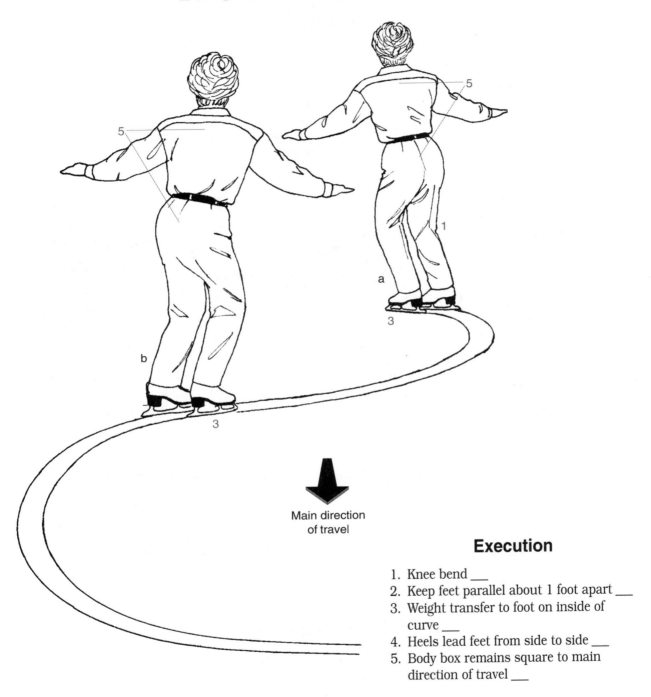

Main direction
of travel

Execution

1. Knee bend ___
2. Keep feet parallel about 1 foot apart ___
3. Weight transfer to foot on inside of curve ___
4. Heels lead feet from side to side ___
5. Body box remains square to main direction of travel ___

FIGURE
5.4 **KEYS TO SUCCESS**

BACKWARD TEETER-TOTTER PUSHES (FROM STANDSTILL)

Prepare to Push

1. Knees bent and feet slightly pigeon-toed ___
2. Shift weight to pushing foot ___
3. Lift future gliding foot off the ice ___
4. Keep lifted foot forward, pigeon-toed, and parallel to ice ___
5. Keep lifted foot close to skating foot (close thighs) ___

Weight Transfer and Glide

6. Place lifted foot on the ice close to pushing foot ___
7. Immediately lift pushing foot (light switch principle) ___
8. Balance weight on gliding foot by tilting free side of body box up ___

Transition to Next Push

9. Increase pressure on inside edge of skating foot ___
10. Shift weight in direction of lifted foot (shift body box) ___

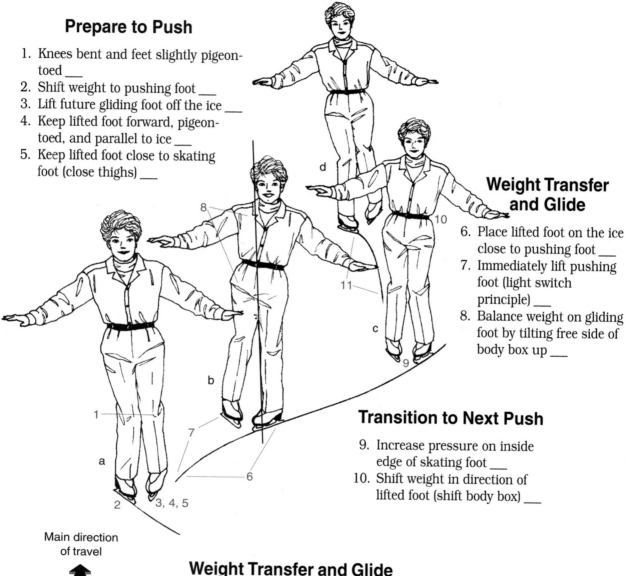

Main direction of travel

Weight Transfer and Glide

11. Place lifted foot on the ice close to pushing foot ___
12. Immediately lift pushing foot (light switch principle) ___
13. Repeat keys 8 through 12.

FIGURE
5.5 **KEYS TO SUCCESS**

SUSTAINED BACKWARD ONE-FOOT GLIDE

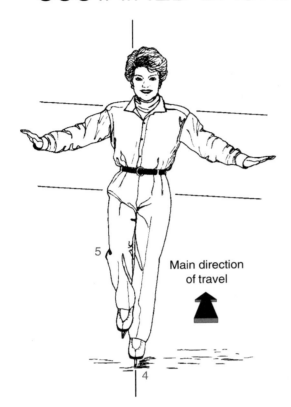

Main direction
of travel

Preparation

1. Gain backward speed ___
2. Two-foot glide with proper skating posture ___

Execution

3. Shift weight to one foot by tilting body box ___
4. Weight over ball of foot ___
5. Lift other foot by bringing your knee up and forward ___

How to Execute Backward Stroking

Once you can sustain backward one-foot glides, try extending your skills with teeter-totter pushes to obtain stronger pushes and more speed. The essence of a strong push is a deep knee bend that adds pressure on the inside edge of the pushing blade (see Figure 5.6). As with all pushes, the light switch principle is in effect. The backward stroking push is usually to a backward outside edge. Transfer your weight onto the ball of your foot and not the heel of the blade. The degree of curvature of the glide path depends on the severity of the outside edge. To help you get a deeper outside edge and a shorter radius of curvature, turn your head toward the center of the curve. Because the push is more vigorous, your free leg extends in front of your gliding foot. At the completion of the push or thrust, your free leg comes off the ice by lifting your free hip. Lifting your free hip causes the necessary body box tilt to put your body weight over your skating foot. Bring your thighs close together immediately after the push (see Figures 5.6c and h) so that the weight of your leg extended away from the body axis does not cause your free hip to drop. Keep your thighs together, your free foot slightly pigeon-toed, and your knees bent throughout the glide. In preparation for the next push, bring your free foot back to your skating foot and keep it there in a pigeon-toed position (see Figure 5.6e). Because all pushes are from an inside edge, you now have to change from an outside edge to an inside edge with your free foot still off the ice (see Figure 5.6f). The transition from outside to inside edge is achieved by straightening your body box tilt over your skating foot to horizontal. At the same time you shift your weight and tilt your body box, turn your head into the new skating direction. After the push, your body box tilt will be to the opposite direction, over your new skating foot (see Figure 5.6g). The overall pattern is a zigzag along the main direction of travel with your pushes at the end of each zigzag leg.

FIGURE
5.6 **KEYS TO SUCCESS**

BACKWARD STROKING
The Initial Push

1. Pick up future gliding foot by lifting the knee forward and slightly in front of other leg keeping the thighs closed ___
2. Shift sternum over toes of pushing foot ___
3. Keep body box alignment ___
4. Increase pressure on inside edge of pushing blade with a slight increase in knee bend ___
5. To thrust, shift your weight to the direction of travel while simultaneously straightening your pushing leg ___
6. Place gliding foot on the ice on an outside edge with sternum aligned over toes on bent knee ___
7. Pushing foot is picked up off the ice by lifting your hip and shoulder on the free side of your body box ___
8. Body box remains facing in the main direction of travel ___

The Backward Outside Glide

9. Close thighs with free leg foot pigeon-toed and toes over the tracing ___
10. Keep free hip and shoulder up with sternum over toes ___

Preparation and Transition to Next Thrust

11. Bring free foot toes to the toes of your gliding foot ___
12. Keep knee bend ___
13. Keep future gliding foot off the ice ___
14. Start shifting weight to new gliding direction to change gliding from an outside to an inside edge ___
15. Increase pressure on inside edge of gliding foot ___
16. Thrust as shown in b and c ___

Gliding On the Opposite Foot

17. Same as in c and d (note that thighs are slightly open after thrust in g and closed in h) ___

How to Execute the Backward Snowplow Stop

There is really only one consistently effective backward stop: the one-sided, backward snowplow stop. This stop uses the same principle as forward snowplow stops (see Figure 5.7). Begin by gliding backward on two feet. Unweigh your stopping foot and turn it to an angle on the ice to produce a skid, and thus a stop. Since the general skating direction is now backward, your stopping foot must be turned out, not pigeon-toed. At the beginning of the stop, there is no body weight on your stopping foot, only the weight of that leg. While maintaining a constant knee bend, shift your weight to your stopping foot. By increasing pressure onto the blade of your stopping foot, you can control whether you come to a standstill or just slow down. As you're stopping, make sure the blade of your stopping foot stays as flat and upright as possible and your body box remains square to your direction of travel (center of back over tracing).

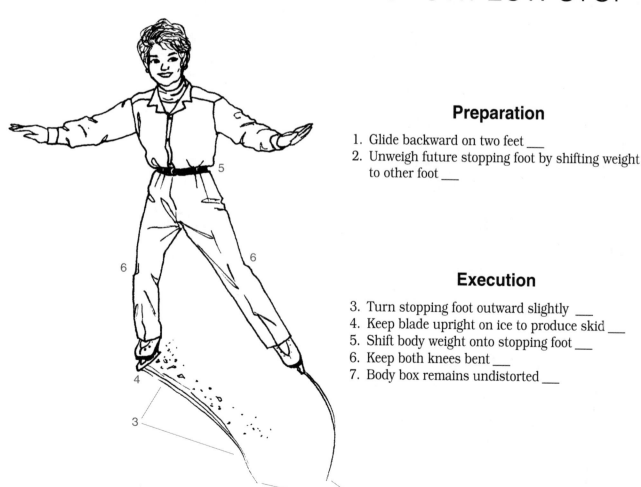

FIGURE 5.7 **KEYS TO SUCCESS**

ONE-SIDED BACKWARD SNOWPLOW STOP

Preparation

1. Glide backward on two feet ___
2. Unweigh future stopping foot by shifting weight to other foot ___

Execution

3. Turn stopping foot outward slightly ___
4. Keep blade upright on ice to produce skid ___
5. Shift body weight onto stopping foot ___
6. Keep both knees bent ___
7. Body box remains undistorted ___

BACKWARD SKATING AND STOPPING SUCCESS STOPPERS

The most common error in backward skating is leaning backward as you try to glide in that direction. This is dangerous and scary but also easily avoided. As your body gets more familiar with the basic skating posture (sternum in line over your toes), you may not find it necessary to think about it constantly. However, because going backward is a new skill, you'll want to be especially conscious of your knee bend and make sure to keep your weight on the balls of your feet or foot.

Error	Correction
Push Off the Wall	
1. Your backward glide curves to one side.	1. You have too much weight on the foot on the side of the curve. Distribute your weight evenly.
2. Your feet tend to glide apart.	2. You put your weight on too much of an inside edge. Keep your blades upright and your feet close and parallel.
3. Your feet collide.	3. You place your weight too much on the outside edges. Keep your blades upright and your feet close and parallel.
Backward Swizzles	
1. You rock back and forth with the upper part of your body box (shoulders).	1. This produces a very unsteady ride. Tightening your abdominal muscles helps keep the correct skating posture stable.
2. Your blade skids rather than gliding.	2. Bend your knees, not your ankles, to get an inside edge. Bending your knees also helps produce speed.
3. Your swizzles are short, fat, and you don't gain speed.	3. Your separating and closing angles of the blades are too steep. Angle your blades to a degree that will produce long and slender shaped tracings.
Backward Teeter-Totter Pushes	
1. You *step* backward instead of gliding backward.	1. Your lifted foot should be placed next to your pushing foot.
2. You feel like you are falling backward as you pick up your free leg.	2. This common error is caused by using your upper body as a counterbalance for lifting one leg. Maintain the basic skating posture with your sternum over the toes of your gliding foot.
3. You have difficulty transferring weight from one foot to the other.	3. You are probably letting your feet slide too far apart. Keep your feet close together.
4. You swing side-to-side with uncontrolled curves which tend to become worse with each step.	4. This is caused by rotating the body box with each step; keep your back toward the main direction of travel. Maintain the basic skating posture.

Error	Correction
Backward One-Foot Glide	
1. You lean backward as you pick up your free foot.	1. This can cause the skating blade to slide away from underneath you. Keep your sternum over the toes of your skating foot and your arms slightly forward.
2. You distort your body box, such as lifting your hip while dropping your shoulder, or vice-versa.	2. To sustain a one-foot glide, your weight must be on top of your skating foot with the skating axis passing from that foot through the opposite shoulder for balance.
3. Your arms are too far back.	3. This brings your shoulders back behind the heel of your skating foot, which upsets your balance.
4. You move your arms, legs, or body box in jerky, reflex-like movements.	4. Avoid excess body movements of any kind. Remember that every action creates an equal and opposite reaction. This can create a domino effect on ice that cannot be stopped easily.
Backward Snowplow Stop	
1. Your stopping foot glides behind you rather than skidding to a stop.	1. Your stopping blade is on too much of an inside edge. Keep your blade upright so it will skid. Keep both knees bent.
2. You trip over the outside edge of your stopping foot.	2. This is rare but can result from a lack of control of your ankle and putting too much weight on your stopping foot too soon. Keep the blade upright.
3. Your body box is twisted as you stop.	3. Keep your shoulders and hips aligned and the center of your back over the tracing.

BACKWARD SKATING AND STOPPING

DRILLS

1. Push Off the Rink Barrier

At first you may not be able to gain or maintain sufficient backward speed to learn moves such as the backward swizzle and wiggle. Try to produce speed by pushing off the rink barrier. This allows you to concentrate on the physical part of the maneuver without worrying about gaining speed.

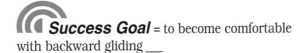**Success Goal** = to become comfortable with backward gliding ___

**Success Check**
• Keep your feet close together and parallel ___
• Proper skating posture ___
• Body weight over your skates ___

2. Backward Swizzles

Begin by trying to maintain the speed gained by the push off the barrier with swizzles. Slowly force your heels apart to about hip width. Then gradually bring your heels back together again. Keep your body box square to the skating direction and your arms extended within your peripheral vision at waist level.

Success Goal = use swizzles to maintain speed gained by the push off ___

Success Check
• Use deepest knee bend when heels are farthest apart ___
• Toes in slight pigeon-toed position ___
• Tracing should show a long, slender, hourglass shape ___

To Increase Difficulty
• Alternately do a series of backward two-foot glides with swizzles.
• Use swizzles to gain speed.

3. Backward Wiggles

Wiggles are another way to maintain the speed you've gained through the push off the barrier. Keep both blades on the ice. Transfer your weight from one side to the other by bending the leg on the inside of the curve slightly more than the other leg.

Success Goal = use wiggles to maintain speed gained by the push off ___

Success Check
• All movement should be from your waist down ___
• Heels turn alternately along "S" shaped tracings ___

To Increase Difficulty
• Use backward wiggles to gain speed.
• Do a series of swizzles and transition into an equal number of wiggles and then reverse the sequence.

4. Teeter-Totter Pushes

The teeter-totter is a preparation for backward stroking and teaches you to transfer weight from one foot to the other. From a standstill position, place your feet slightly pigeon-toed with your big toes almost touching. Apply pressure to the inside edge of your pushing foot and push, lift that knee, and let your weight center over your gliding foot. Then repeat with your other foot to the opposite side. Keep your body box square to the main direction of travel.

Success Goal = do backward teeter-totter pushes to gain speed from a standstill ___

Success Check
• Push from the inside edge of your pushing foot ___
• Keep weight over your skating foot ___
• Zigzag tracings result from longer glides ___

To Increase Difficulty
• Apply more pressure to lengthen your glides and speed.

To Decrease Difficulty
• Start from a push off the barrier.

5. Backward One-Sided Snowplow Stop

The backward stop should be learned now before you progress further. Begin by doing this backward stop immediately after a push off the barrier. When you're comfortable with this, perform the stop after a series of wiggles and swizzles, especially when you're able to gain speed with these maneuvers.

Success Goal =
a. to stop in a considerably shorter distance than was required to gain speed ___
b. to predetermine a specific place to stop on the rink, approach it with the greatest amount of speed you can achieve and control, and stop there ___

Success Check
• Unweigh future stopping foot by shifting weight to your other foot ___
• Turn stopping foot slightly outward ___
• Keep both knees bent ___

6. Backward One-Foot Glide

When you can do Drill 5 without a push off the barrier, use backward wiggles, swizzles, or teeter-totter pushes to gain enough speed to sustain a backward one-foot glide (remember that balance is aided by speed).

Success Goal = to hold a one-foot glide for at least a distance equal to your height with as few wiggles or swizzles as possible to gain the necessary speed ___

Success Check
• Tilt body box slightly over your skating foot ___
• Feet remain parallel ___

To Increase Difficulty
• Add a backward snowplow stop at the end of your extended glide.

To Decrease Difficulty
• Barely lift other foot off the ice.

7. Backward Stroking

Begin with a few teeter-totter pushes and then increase the pressure of the pushes and the length of the glides so that you are now doing backward strokes. Then experiment with short and rapid backward strokes that gain speed quickly. Maintain speed with a slower stroke frequency and longer glides between each push.

Success Goal = to hold balance during the glide with the slower stroke for a distance equal at least to your height ___

Success Check
• Push from an inside edge ___
• Transfer weight to a backward outside edge near the ball of your foot ___
• Turn your head toward the skating direction ___

To Increase Difficulty
• Practice snowplow stops with the above exercises at varying speeds.

To Decrease Difficulty
• Practice at a comfortable speed.

BACKWARD SKATING AND STOPPING SUCCESS SUMMARY

Backward skating challenges your ability to balance and gain speed in new ways. The same principles of forward skating apply to backward skating. Virtually all of the principles and maneuvers introduced for forward skating in Steps 1, 2, and 4 and the snowplow stop from Step 3 have a backward counterpart. A trained observer should judge your progress with the maneuvers of this step using the checklists in Figures 5.1 through 5.7. Ask the observer to also check that your body box is aligned, your posture correct (sternum over toes), and your knees bent.

The Rideau Canal with the Canadian Parliament buildings in the background, Ottawa, Ontario. The Rideau Canal is the world's longest maintained skating rink. Six kilometers (4 miles) are kept clear and smooth and provided with heated huts, food concessions, and skate-sharpening and rental services.
This drawing has been adapted from a painting by Inge Claussen.

STEP 6

FORWARD STROKING: PUSHING FOR POWER

I n this step you'll learn to use your legs to stroke forward with efficiency and power to gain and maintain maximum speed. This is a major step forward in your skating skills. As your strength and confidence increase, so will the speed you can attain.

We begin this step by reintroducing the light switch principle, which we first discussed in Step 2. We'll explain in detail the mechanics of the principle and its relation to power pushes.

The second component of the power push is the resulting glide. Earlier, just gliding was the success goal. In this step, we'll fine tune your gliding technique. We'll work on finishing a power push with an extended glide on either a forward outside or forward inside edge. Ultimately, it doesn't matter whether you stroke onto an outside or inside edge, as both will give sufficient speed. You'll find a favorite, but at present you should learn both.

To do these pushes with success, you really must control your body box and skating posture. To benefit fully from the mechanics presented here, you'll need to eliminate any excuses you've had for distorting your body box in the past.

Why Are Power Pushes Onto Edges Important?

Forward stroking onto either an inside or an outside edge is the advanced way of skating forward with power and speed. Inside edge stroking produces long curves which begin and end on the center line of the main direction of forward travel. Outside edge stroking will generate a zigzag pattern that crosses the center line in the middle of the stroke. The inside stroke produces a flowing motion on the ice and is often preferred by freestyle skaters. The outside stroke is crisper and used often in compulsory dances and speed skating. Since all pushes are done from an inside edge, when the pre-push glide is on an outside edge, you'll learn to switch to an inside edge to do your next push.

Why should you push onto an edge rather than onto the flat of the blade? First, gliding on an edge is much more secure than on the flat of the blade and helps you maintain balance. There is an old saying among ice skaters: "Find the security of an edge." Second, gliding on one edge results in less resistance between the skate and the ice: Gliding on the flat of the blade presses both edges and the hollow of the blade to the ice, increasing resistance. Third, stroking onto an edge with each push is natural because of the body lean that accompanies each push.

How to Execute the Power Push

The mechanics of stroking are the same from a standstill and at full speed. Only the distances between your pushing foot and your striking foot vary. The mechanism of weight transfer from the pushing foot to the gliding foot is so fundamental to ice skating that it is itself a basic principle. This third basic principle we have designated the "light switch principle." Accordingly, the weight is solely on the pushing foot as that leg is straightened. Thus, except for a fraction of a second, all of the weight is either on the thrusting foot or the gliding foot. Four factors underlie efficient, powerful stroking no matter what edge or direction a stroke takes. First, the push is always done with an inside edge (see Figure 2.1, p. 22). The way the blade contacts the ice determines the effectiveness of the transfer of force from your thrusting leg to the ice. Second, your weight is only on your pushing foot as your pushing leg is straightened (light switch "on"). Your free foot remains off the ice and at an angle to your pushing foot until almost full leg extension occurs (see Figure 6.1). The degree of the angle will depend on the speed and how flat the curve of the ensuing glide will be. With the completion of the thrust, your free foot contacts the ice and becomes your gliding foot. Simultaneously, you lift your pushing foot off the ice (light switch "off"), placing all your weight on your gliding foot. For the most effi-

cient stroking, your pushing leg is lifted only a few inches off the ice. Third, just as crucial as the way the pushing blade contacts the ice is the knee bend of your pushing leg, as it determines the power of each stroke. Fourth, except for extension of your pushing leg at the end of the thrust, keep both knees bent so that your hips remain at a constant height above the ice. If a light were placed on the top of your head in a dark ice rink, it should trace a line continuously parallel to the ice surface, without up and down oscillations.

<table>
<tr><td>FIGURE
6.1</td><td>**KEYS TO SUCCESS**</td></tr>
</table>

FORWARD POWER PUSH

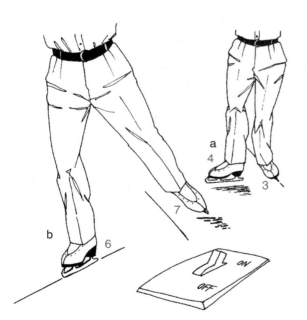

Principle #3:
Light Switch Off

1. Basic skating posture ___
2. Knees bent ___
3. Full weight on inside edge of pushing foot, front one-third of blade ___
4. Other foot off the ice and angled away from your pushing foot ___

Principle #3:
Light Switch On

5. Thrust your body forward by straightening pushing leg ___
6. Weight transfer must be completed when gliding foot strikes the ice (sternum over toes of gliding foot) ___
7. Pushing foot is lifted off the ice at instant gliding foot strikes the ice (light switch principle) ___

How to Execute Forward Inside Edge Stroking

With both inside and outside edge forward stroking, your body box remains square to the main direction of travel (see Figure 6.2a). For glides on an inside edge, the angle of your striking foot places it in line under your armpit (Figure 6.2b). To help you strike the ice on an inside edge, your ankle should be slightly bent inward—this happens almost automatically. The distance between your pushing foot and where your striking foot contacts the ice will vary depending on your speed and degree of knee bend. To transfer your body weight smoothly from one foot to the other, your sternum must remain forward in line with your knee and your toes of your striking foot (Figure 6.2c). As your striking foot contacts the ice, pick up your pushing foot. If your free leg is lifted too high in the back, you'll spend too much time retrieving it. For efficient speed skating, keep the extended free foot only an inch or so above the ice. For style or to help strengthen your gluteal and lower back muscles, you can lift your back leg higher. After the push, the heel of your free leg should stay over the tracing (Figures 6.2b and c). For the next push, bring your free leg forward by bending and pulling your knee forward (Figure 6.2d). As you bring your foot forward to the instep of your gliding foot, keep the blade as parallel to the ice

as possible (Figures 6.2a and e). Now the procedure can begin again. The pattern produced by this kind of stroking results in consecutive curves that end on or near the main line of travel. The depth of the curves, the rate of stroking, and the speed are personal preferences and will depend on your skill level.

How to Execute Forward Outside Edge Stroking

The knee bend, thrust, and weight transfer are the same as with the inside edge stroke. The main difference is that your striking foot hits an outside edge upon contacting the ice. To anticipate striking and to maintain the outside edge, keep your head turned toward the direction of travel of your gliding foot. The pattern created by this stroke is a zigzag that crosses the main line of travel (see Figure 6.3). As your free leg is retrieved from its backward extension by bending your knee and bringing it forward, your free ankle must bend outward to enable placement of the blade on an outside edge. For the inside edge, you placed your foot at the moment of the strike in line under your armpit. For striking onto an outside edge, your foot is more in line with your breast. In other words, the angle of your striking foot in relation to your pushing foot and main direction of travel is smaller.

FIGURE
6.2

KEYS TO SUCCESS

FORWARD INSIDE EDGE STROKING

Poised to Push

1. Body box square to main line of travel ___
2. Weight on inside edge of thrusting foot ___
3. Knees bent ___

Weight Transfer and Glide

4. Weight transfer to inside edge of gliding foot (light switch principle) ___
5. Sternum, knee, and toes of gliding foot in line ___
6. Heel of free foot over tracing ___

Leg Retrieval Stage

7. Free leg knee is bent and brought forward ___

Main direction of travel

Poised to Push Again

8. Free foot poised at the instep of gliding foot ___
9. Begin next light switch power push ___

FIGURE
6.3 KEYS TO SUCCESS

FORWARD OUTSIDE EDGE STROKING

Poised to Push

1. Body box square to main line of travel ___
2. Weight on inside edge of thrusting foot ___
3. Knees bent ___
4. Head turned in direction of skating leg ___

Weight Transfer and Glide

5. Weight transfer to outside edge of gliding foot (light switch principle) ___
6. Sternum, knee, and toes of gliding foot in line ___
7. Heel of free foot over tracing ___

Main direction of travel

Leg Retrieval Stage

8. Free leg knee is bent and brought forward ___

Poised to Push Again

9. Repeat ___

FORWARD STROKING SUCCESS STOPPERS

The errors and corrections for pushes to outside and inside edges are essentially the same because the light switch push is the same for both. The keys to success are the pressure on the inside edge of the pushing foot and the weight transfer to the gliding foot—thus, the main errors are in these two aspects of the push and glide.

Error	Correction
1. You lean backward as you bring your striking foot forward making it difficult to transfer weight onto the gliding foot.	1. All motion should occur below your waist. The front of your chest, your knees, and your toes should always remain in line.
2. You move up and down by inadvertently straightening your skating knee when your free leg is straightened.	2. Your body should remain at a constant level above the ice. Keep your skating leg bent.
3. You rotate your body box rather than maintaining it facing the main direction of travel.	3. Keep the heel of your extended foot over the tracing and keep your sternum over your gliding toes.
4. As your weight transfers onto your gliding foot, the weight is placed in line with your foot and knee but not with the hip, which is pushed outward. This occurs when you place your gliding foot too far to the side of your pushing foot.	4. To get your gliding foot, knee, and hip aligned under your body weight, keep your feet close together to ease weight transfer from one foot to the other.
5. When you retrieve your free leg after the full extension of the push, you catch your toepick on the ice.	5. This often occurs when you are trying to impress someone with your speed. Be sure to keep your free skate blade parallel to the ice.

FORWARD STROKING

DRILLS

1. Power Pushes

To familiarize yourself more with power pushes, concentrate on the following four factors for this first exercise. Those components which make up the power push will at first require four different thought processes which must occur in chronological order. Ultimately, they will be committed to muscle memory. They are in order: Push from the inside edge and the front one-third of the blade; transfer weight in the light switch fashion; remain on a bent knee; and, straighten your free leg (pushing leg) at the end of the thrust to its full extension and hold its heel over the tracing.

Success Goal = to achieve a smooth push and weight transfer into a balanced glide ___

To Increase Difficulty
• Do fewer strokes and cover more ice.

Success Check
• Both knees stay bent ___
• Hips and shoulders remain at a constant height above ice ___
• Thrusting leg is lifted only a few inches off the ice ___

2. Forward Inside Edge Stroking

Inside edge stroking produces long, concave curves that begin and end on the center line of the main direction of forward travel. With each power push transfer your weight onto an inside edge for your one-foot glide. Transfer body weight smoothly from one foot to the other. Extend your arms to your sides within your peripheral vision for balance. Keep your sternum forward in line with your knee and your toes of each striking foot. Maintain your glide equally on both sides to create symmetrical consecutive curves.

Success Goal = to create mirror image concave patterns with each foot ___

To Increase Difficulty
• Vary the tempo of pushes and glides.

To Decrease Difficulty
• Stroke in time to music to improve your rhythm and for enjoyment.

Success Check
• Body box remains square to main line of travel ___
• Weight transfer to inside edge ___
• Concave curve pattern ___

3. Forward Outside Edge Stroking

Outside edge stroking generates a zigzag pattern that crosses the center line in the middle of the stroke. Take your normal power push from an inside edge. Transfer your weight onto the outside edge of your gliding foot. Turn your head toward the direction of travel of your gliding foot. The angle of your striking foot in relation to your pushing foot and main direction of travel should be smaller than that used during your forward inside edge stroking.

Success Goal = to create mirror image, zigzag patterns with each foot ___

Success Check
- Body box remains square to main line of travel ___
- Weight transfer to outside edge ___
- Zigzag pattern ___

To Increase Difficulty
- Vary the tempo of pushes and glides.

To Decrease Difficulty
- Stroke in time to music to improve your rhythm and for enjoyment.

4. Forward Stroking With Stops

Your stopping skills must remain equal to the level of your skating skills. In previous exercises you have already practiced snowplow stops. To practice and familiarize yourself with hockey and T-stops, combine them with inside and outside forward stroking. From a standstill, take five outside or inside forward strokes. Apply as much pressure on your pushing foot as possible to gain maximum speed. Stop with a hockey stop on alternate sides. For figure skaters, practice T-stops also to both sides.

Success Goal = to stop in a significantly shorter distance than the distance traveled taking the five strokes ___

Success Check
- Use power pushes ___
- Stop with control ___

To Increase Difficulty
- Combine any two (or more) skills introduced so far prior to your stop.
- Try both sides and directions when applicable.

To Decrease Difficulty
- Combine any two skills at your discretion and pleasure before any stop.

5. Power Pushes Into an Extended One-Foot Glide

To test your ability to generate speed with very few pushes, limit the number of pushes, such as five or even three, and continue gliding for as long as you can on one foot. Begin at a stand-still. Perform your pushes. For the extended glide, no particular edge is necessary—in fact, the flat of the blade will give you a straighter course.

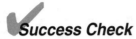 **Success Goal** = to glide on one foot a greater distance than that required to gain speed ___

Success Check

- Use power pushes ___
- Maintain balance in extended glide ___

To Increase Difficulty

- Use fewer pushes to obtain the same glide distance.
- Attempt to glide the entire length of the rink.

FORWARD STROKING SUCCESS SUMMARY

Because errors are so easily recognized in this step, you may not need a trained observer to help. A fellow beginning skater can help judge your success. Ask him or her to rate your progress according to the checklists in Figures 6.1 through 6.3. Signs of abnormalities with these keys will express themselves by rocking back and forth, up and down movements, and twisting and distortion of your body box. Ask your observer to tell you whether or not you have such problems.

A warm spring morning at the Winter Lodge, Palo Alto, California.

STEP 7
FORWARD CROSSOVERS: STROKING ON A CURVE

I f there's one group of competitive skaters who stand above the rest in gaining speed faster and with seemingly very little effort, it is the Russian pairs skaters. It is clear why the Russians have so often become champions: they are able to gain great speed with very few strokes, in addition to performing all of the complex maneuvers. Their key to success, particularly when stroking on a curve, was a well guarded secret for many years. We choose to call this secret *body box rotation.* Body box rotation combined with a deep knee bend promotes a lean into the curve being skated. This allows you to concentrate the centrifugal force created by skating on a curve directly onto the edge of the blade. It also allows you to obtain a steeper angle of the blade relative to the ice and a longer leg extension with each push. This in combination with the light switch principle will give you the potential to gain just as much speed. In this step you'll be introduced to skating on a curve that will be used to interconnect straight line skating sequences and can be used to skate in circles. Power stroking on a curve is your goal. To get to this goal, you'll be taken step by step from skateboard pushes through beginner crossovers to advanced crossovers.

Why Are Forward Crossovers Important?

Skateboard pushes create speed on a curve by pushing with one leg. In contrast, the advantage of crossovers is that both legs are used to push and, therefore, the potential to gain more speed is at least twice as great. Beginner crossovers will enable you to learn the basic movements at a controlled speed. Only a slight modification will result in advanced crossovers and a lot more power and speed.

The Secret of Body Box Rotation

Rotation of your body box so that it faces toward the inside of the curve is done to obtain stability and power while stroking along a curve. It will also be used to gain stability and control of body movements in turns of any type. The rotation and lean are always toward the inside of the curve independent of the edge of your skating foot or the direction, such as forward or backward. Rotation of your body box and lean into the circle allow you to concentrate the combined force of your body weight and centrifugal force created by skating on a curve onto the edges of your skate blades without being thrown out of the curve. It is analogous to the lean of a bicycle on a curve that helps it turn. You'll find that maximum stability and power when skating on a curve are achieved when your hips and shoulders are rotated into the curve equally and, conversely, you'll find less control and power when your shoulders are rotated more than your hips.

How to Execute Body Box Rotation

Begin by prerotating your body box to face toward the inside of the curve to be skated (see Figure 7.1a). Note that your hips and shoulders should be rotated equally and line up parallel with the skating direction. Under no circumstances should your body box be broken or twisted by having your shoulders or hips rotate to different degrees. Beginners often find that they can rotate their shoulders but cannot rotate their hips to the same degree. A deep knee bend helps to achieve correct rotation of both elements of your body box. With rotation of your body box, the center of your sternum shifts from being directly over your skating foot toes to a point inside the curve being skated. This shift in the relationship of your sternum to your skating foot in combination with body box rotation when skating on a curve is the fourth basic principle of skating, which we call "the medallion principle" (see Figures 7.1b and c). The distance between the skate and the point within the curve will vary depending on the speed and the size of the curve. With faster speeds and tighter curves, the lean into the circle will be greater. To help understand this principle, imagine a medallion hanging around your neck. If you lean to the inside of the curve, the medallion would hang free and point to the spot on the ice alongside the skating foot, directly under your sternum.

FIGURE 7.1 **KEYS TO SUCCESS**

BODY BOX ROTATION
Principle #4:
The Medallion Principle

1. Equal degree of rotation of hips and shoulders toward center of curve to be skated ___
2. Sternum over a point next to your skating foot on the inside of the curve ___
3. Bend knees ___

How to Execute Skateboard Pushes

Skateboard pushes consist of gliding on one foot while pushing repetitively with the other. This is the first exercise in which your body box is rotated to help you skate on a curve. It will help you experience the advantage of body box rotation and lean without having to do crossovers. Begin by prerotating your body box to face toward the inside of the curve to be skated (see Figure 7.2a). For skateboard pushes, your body weight is supported mainly by your skating foot on a slightly bent knee and on an outside edge. In this case, your skating foot is the one to the inside of the curve. The only time that your weight is not fully supported by your skating foot is during the push. Your push is done repetitively with your outside foot using the front one-third of its inside edge (see Figure 2.1). As with all forward pushes, extension of your leg is at about a 45-degree angle to your side and back.

The skateboard push begins with both knees bent and the pushing (outside) foot next to your skating (inside) foot (see Figure 7.2a). At the completion of the push, your pushing foot is fully extended and is lifted off the ice (see Figure 7.2b). Note that full extension of your pushing leg indicates that a full length thrust was achieved. A slight distortion of your body box may occur if the free leg is extended to an extreme back position. For your next thrust, your pushing leg is returned by bending your knee and lifting it forward close to your skating knee (see Figure 7.2c). Your pushing foot is placed on the ice immediately next to your skating foot on an inside edge in preparation for your next thrust (see Figure 7.2d). That thrust is completed when your pushing leg is fully extended (see Figure 7.2e). Note that for each part of the skateboard stroke, your body box remains rotated, your sternum remains over a point to the side of your skating foot, and the knee bend of your skating foot remains constant.

How to Execute Beginner Forward Crossovers

For every kind of crossover, forward or backward, your body box is rotated so that your shoulders and your hips face toward the center of the circle. Your head is turned so that you're looking in the skating direction. Your arms are held midway between your hips and shoulders to help you keep your balance and, as a general rule, are held along the direction of the tracing made by the skates. Push with your outside leg as described in skateboard pushes. After the push is completed and your free leg is extended fully, bend your knee and lift it forward. Keep the blade parallel to the ice and your free hip up (see Figure 7.3a). To cross your free leg from the outside to the inside of the circle, close the upper part of your thighs (see Figure 7.3b). It is important to keep your toe of your free foot turned toward the center of the circle (pigeon-toed) and your knee bent so that an inside edge is achieved immediately upon impact with the ice (see Figure 7.3c). Your knee remains bent throughout the lifting across your skating foot. Note, your free foot is placed within a few inches of your skating foot and at about the same level (little toe to little toe). Because most of your body weight shifts to your crossing foot, little thrust can be expected from your back foot. Try to maintain a glide on both feet for at least a short distance in this crossed-foot position. The crossover is completed at this point. You now have to prepare for the next thrust forward. To pick up the crossed back foot from the ice, lift its knee forward and upward (see Figure 7.3d) keeping the blade parallel to the ice as much as possible and close to your skating leg (note, your skating leg is now the leg on the outside of the circle). At this point, you have reached the beginning of the sequence again. You push backward at about a 45-degree angle with your outside foot until full extension of your thrusting leg is attained (see Figure 7.3e). While your outside leg is pushing backward, your inside foot is held just above the ice (review Figure 6.1, p. 64, the light switch principle). Simultaneous with full extension of your thrusting leg, your other foot is placed on the ice on an outside edge and your thrusting leg is lifted off the ice (see Figure 7.3f). When done correctly, your body box is tilted toward the inside of the circle. This causes your outside hip and shoulder to be higher than the inside. Maintaining your outside hip up throughout this maneuver is essential to keep your weight off the outside edge of the skate on the inside of the circle.

FIGURE
7.2

KEYS TO SUCCESS

SKATEBOARD PUSHES
Medallion Principle

1. Body box rotation and lean ___
2. Knees bent ___
3. Arms extended over tracing to be skated ___

Inside Edge Push

4. Push with front one-third of inside edge of blade ___
5. Fully extend pushing leg ___

Leg Retrieval

6. Bring pushing knee forward and upward next to skating knee ___

Preparation for Next Push

7. Place pushing foot next to skating foot ___

Completion of Push

8. Repeat the skateboard push ___

FIGURE
7.3

KEYS TO SUCCESS

BEGINNER FORWARD CROSSOVERS
Crossover

1. Body box rotation and lean into circle ___
2. Knees bent ___
3. Cross outside foot over your skating foot keeping thighs together ___

Retrieval of Back Foot

4. Place your crossing foot on the ice on an inside edge without lifting your other foot ___
5. Most of your body weight is placed onto your crossing foot ___
6. Crossing foot knee remains bent ___
7. Hold onto the resulting two-foot glide for a moment ___
8. Lift crossed back knee upward and forward ___

Thrust and Glide

9. Push with outside leg at 45-degree angle ___
10. Keep inside foot off the ice (light switch principle) ___
11. Place inside foot on ice at end of push ___
12. Inside knee is bent ___
13. Inside blade is on an outside edge ___

How to Execute Advanced Forward Crossovers (Forward Crossunders)

Advanced crossovers use many of the same techniques that you learned in beginner crossovers. For example, the initial push is the same (see Figure 7.4a). As your outside free foot is brought forward after the end of the thrust it is placed on the ice at the same level as the inside skate (see Figure 7.4b). Your outside foot does not leave the ice until the end of the crossover sequence. The main difference is that in the beginner crossover, your foot is lifted across your skating foot to achieve a crossing. In the advanced form, the crossover is achieved by pushing your inside leg under (see Figures 7.4c and d). This push creates as much speed as the initial thrust. The value of advanced crossovers is that both legs are able to push with equal force and the movement is much smoother. The deeper the knee bend of your inside leg, the greater the distance between the inside and outside foot, which creates a longer distance to the crossunder point and therefore more power. The length of time your outside leg spends thrusting to a fully extended position and the inside spends crossing under and fully extending should be equal. When full extension is reached, the foot that was crossed under is lifted off the ice and brought next to your skating foot by bending your knee upward and forward (see Figures 7.4e and f). Because of the deeper knee bend, there will be an increase in speed, an increased lean into the circle, and more pressure on the edges of the blades during the thrusts.

Advantages of the "Crossunder" Concept

One of the main differences between beginner and advanced crossovers is the degree of lean of your body box into the circle. Because the outside skate must be lifted over the inside skate with beginner crossovers, the skater's body must be held more erect whereas a greater lean into the circle and deeper inside leg knee bend can be achieved with the advanced form (compare Figures 7.5a and d). The difference in body lean will also influence the power of the stroke with the outside leg because, although the thrusts are similar, due to the degree of knee bend they are different in length. The main advantage of the advanced crossover is the length of its crossunder stroke, which is at least 2 times longer than the beginner form (compare Figures 7.5a, b, and c with d, e, and f).

FIGURE
7.4

KEYS TO SUCCESS

ADVANCED FORWARD CROSSOVERS
Outside Edge Glide

1. Body box rotation and lean into circle ___
2. Continuous knee bend for leg supporting weight ___

Outside Edge Thrust

3. Place outside foot on inside edge ___
4. Bend both knees during thrust ___
5. Extend crossunder leg fully ___

Inside Edge Thrust

6. Pick crossed knee upward and forward ___
7. Simultaneously, push with outside leg at 45-degree angle ___
8. Keep inside foot off ice until end of thrust (light switch principle) ___

Figure 7.5 Comparison of beginner (a, b, c) and advanced (d, e, f) crossovers. Note the differences in body lean, edge, knee bend, and length of crossunder strokes (arrows).

FORWARD CROSSOVERS SUCCESS STOPPERS

Detecting errors in your performance of this step may be as easy as feeling your toepicks catch because of stiff knees, an inability to gain speed, or a twisted feeling that leaves you seemingly without control. In our opinion, it may be very helpful at this time to watch other skaters. Some will probably be struggling like you whereas others seem to glide almost effortlessly. Obviously, the skill level of the observed skater has a great deal to do with the skater's appearance. With the information given in this step, it should be possible for you to identify some errors or their absence.

Error	Correction
Body Box Rotation	
1. You rotate your shoulders significantly more than your hips.	1. Turn your hips and shoulders to the same degree, facing the inside of the circle. Line up your armpit directly over your hip.
2. You stand too upright with your sternum still over your feet.	2. The plane of your body box must be turned to face the inside of the circle and must lean forward into the circle, bringing your sternum over a point to the side of your foot.
3. You don't bend your knees enough.	3. The degree of knee bend needed to get both hips and shoulders to rotate equally will vary from person to person. Knee bend is required to develop a solid, powerful push.
Skateboard Pushes and Forward Crossovers	
1. You push with your toepicks.	1. Toepick pushes may seem to give you more thrust at first, but they usually cause your free hip to drop, which creates problems. Use the front one-third of the inside edge of the skate blade (see Figure 2.1).
2. Your arms and/or body box counterrotates with each push often causing a backward lean.	2. Keep your hands and arms extended on top of the tracing carved by your skating foot and the center of your chest (sternum) leaning into the circle (medallion principle).
3. Your gliding foot is incorrectly placed on an inside edge or fails to be on an edge at all.	3. This makes it impossible to skate on a curve. Adjust the rotation of your body box and position your sternum over a point to the inside of the curve. Your body weight should always be supported by the foot to the inside of the curve and on an outside edge.

(continued)

Error	Correction
Skateboard Pushes and Forward Crossovers (continued)	
4. You drop your outside hip when placing your pushing foot on the ice.	4. If you drop your outside hip, your body box becomes distorted and it is difficult to shift your weight to the other foot. Without proper weight transfer, the inside foot cannot be pushed under effectively. Keep your outside free hip from dropping in combination with rotating your body box into the curve.
5. Your knees are too straight.	5. Bend your knees. If you don't bend your knees during beginner crossovers, you'll have to move your crossing foot around the toepick of your skating foot, which creates rotational momentum from the swing of your free leg and encourages your free hip to drop.

FORWARD CROSSOVERS

DRILLS

1. Prerotated Body Box Position

The more familiar you are with body box rotation the easier it will be for you to not only do forward crossovers but also backward crossovers, mohawks, and three turns that will be introduced to you in upcoming steps. If you're having trouble, stand in front of a mirror at home and check your starting position. Begin by standing sideways to a mirror. Bend your knees. Rotate your body box to face the mirror. Bend your body box forward by bringing your sternum closer to the mirror. To help develop muscle memory of this position, hold for a count of 10. Be sure to check your body box rotation in both directions.

Success Goal = hold rotated body box position for 10 seconds, then repeat to the other side until each side feels comfortable ___

Success Check
- Align knees, hips, and shoulders parallel to the floor (layer cake concept) ___
- Hips and shoulders rotated equally ___
- Body box faces toward the inside of the curve ___

To Increase Difficulty
- Repeat the whole procedure with your eyes closed to help develop the feeling for this position. Then open your eyes and check your position.

To Decrease Difficulty
- Ask a trained partner to check your alignment.

2. Skateboard Pushes on a Curve

Skateboard pushes start with both knees bent. Prerotate your body box. Push with your outside foot until it is extended and slightly off the ice. Bring both feet together again in preparation for the next thrust. Practice curves on both sides.

Success Goal = execute consecutive skateboard pushes on a curve with proper body box rotation and lean to each side ___

Success Check
- Skating foot has a slightly bent knee ___
- Weight on an outside edge ___
- Body box remains rotated ___
- Push with front one-third of outside foot's inside edge ___

To Increase Difficulty
- Execute fewer pushes within the same distance.

To Decrease Difficulty
- Execute more pushes within the same distance.

3. Full Circle Skateboard Pushes

Try to skate a full circle with as few skateboard pushes as possible. The radius of the circle should be about equal to your height. Many beginning skaters go through the motions of the push but don't actually gain speed. Try to reduce the number of pushes required to skate a full circle.

Try five pushes and then skate the remaining part of the circle with a one-foot glide. This drill is important to prepare you for the one-foot gliding necessary to perform crossovers.

Success Goal =
a. to use an equal number of pushes in both directions and to make each portion of the figure identical ___
b. to execute 5 pushes, then a one-foot glide for the remainder of the circle ___

Success Check
- Sternum remains over a point to the side of your skating foot ___
- Arms extend over tracing to be skated ___
- Knee bend of skating foot remains constant ___

To Increase Difficulty
- Do skateboard pushes in one direction and then, without loss of speed, rotate your body box and lean to the opposite direction and skate a figure-8.

To Decrease Difficulty
- Gradually lengthen the amount of time that you glide on one foot.

4. Beginner Crossovers

The most basic drill is to attempt a series of beginner crossovers without extra steps in between to regain balance or to add speed (review Figures 7.3a through f). Refine your technique so that you are equally strong and comfortable in both directions.

Success Goal = to complete 5 consecutive crossovers in both directions ___

Success Check
• Body box is tilted toward inside of the circle ___
• Place crossing foot on the ice on an inside edge without lifting your other foot ___
• Crossing foot knee remains bent ___
• Momentary hold of two-foot glide ___
• Use light switch principle ___

To Increase Difficulty
• Skate the same number of crossovers in a circle in both directions keeping the size of the circles equal.

To Decrease Difficulty
• Gradually increase the number of consecutive crossovers on a curve to both sides.

5. Figure-8s or Consecutive Half-Circles

Two important drills you can do with beginner crossovers but that also apply to advanced crossovers are figure-8s and consecutive half circles. These will force you to practice crossovers to both sides and will really familiarize you with body box rotation and lean into the circle being skated. In addition, they will give you experience making the transition from body box rotation and lean in one direction to the other. The key to success for a smooth transition is to avoid creating upper body rotational momentum. For beginner crossovers, this is accomplished in the following way. At the end of a series of crossovers in one direction, continue gliding on that circle on two feet. Drop your arms next to your sides. Turn your body box to the other side, lean into the curve in the new direction and begin gliding along the opposite circle. Lift your arms along the tracing and begin crossovers in the new direction. Practicing a relatively large number of crossovers in both directions is ideally done as figure-8s. If the conditions at your ice rink make it hard to do figure-8s, do consecutive half-circles in the main flow of traffic.

Success Goal = to execute forward crossovers along a figure-8 path (or consecutive half-circles) ___

Success Check
• Body box tilts toward the inside of the circle ___
• Simultaneous with full extension of the thrusting leg, your other foot is placed on the ice on an outside edge and your thrusting leg lifts off the ice ___

To Increase Difficulty
• Vary the number of strokes and diameters of the figure-8s and/or the half-circles.

To Decrease Difficulty
• Use a few skateboard pushes.

6. Advanced Crossovers

For advanced crossovers, do the same as for beginner crossovers to develop confidence and competence in both directions. The transition between opposite circles in figure-8s and consecutive half-circles can be done on two feet as with beginner crossovers but can also be done on one foot. For the latter, do the following. As you finish a circle or half-circle of crossovers, uncross the foot that has been crossed under and place it on the ice on an inside edge under the center of your sternum to start the new circle. If you place it on an outside edge, you would continue along the old crossover circle. At the start of that inside edge, your arms are still in the same position as the old crossovers even though your body box is square to the direction of travel. To avoid creating extraneous rotational momentum, again drop your arms to your sides. As you lift your arms in a switched fashion, your body box will rotate and lean into the opposite circle. All of this is done while skating on a forward inside edge. Once your body box is facing the inside of the new circle, you are compelled to begin the crossovers.

A beneficial form of "torture" is to hold the inside edge with full extension of your free leg in the crossunder position (see Figure 7.5c) for an extended period of time. This helps develop confidence with this position and strengthens your legs.

Because crossovers are inherently rhythmic, they are well suited for music. In fact, music often enhances their pleasure. Experiment with an equal number of crossovers at different speeds from very fast, somewhat choppy crossovers to long, slow, languid crossovers.

Success Goal = to execute an equal number of advanced crossovers at different speeds to both sides ___

Success Check

- Thrust your inside leg under (review Figures 7.4c and d) ___
- A deeper knee bend of your inside leg generates more power ___
- Increased lean of your body box into the circle ___

FORWARD CROSSOVERS SUCCESS SUMMARY

The two most important concepts covered in this step were body box rotation and lean for skating on a curve and its application to gain and maintain speed. If it seems we have spent an awful lot of time explaining body box rotation, it is because it will be revisited for backward crossovers, three turns, and mohawks as well as many more moves not discussed in this book. Many skating instructors emphasize upper body (shoulder) rotation and do not mention hip rotation for crossovers. However, it is the combination of shoulder and hip rotation that gives the possibility for the lean that will direct centrifugal and body weight forces directly on an edge. Ask your coach or a trained observer to evaluate your performance using the checklists in Figures 7.1 to 7.4.

Crystal clear ice on a High Sierra lake with entrapped air bubbles, Lake Tahoe region, California. This is the artist's interpretation of a Forest Ranger's description of a remote ice skating spot.

STEP 8

TWO-FOOT TURNS AND MOHAWKS: CONTROLLING ROTATION

The most common methods of changing direction from forward to backward are the *two-foot turn* and the *forward inside mohawk*, movements popular with both hockey skaters and figure skaters because they can be performed at either high or low speed. Proper execution of these changes and turns—as well as others we'll discuss in upcoming steps—can potentially create tremendous rotational momentum. While rotational momentum is necessary for spins and jumps, if uncontrolled when you're changing direction, it can be very disruptive.

We begin this step by introducing a fifth basic skating principle: *turning within your arms*. We have found this controls rotational momentum during any kind of directional change or turn. The philosophy of changing direction embodied in this principle is to prerotate those body parts that because of their mass or distance from the rotational axis can create extra rotational momentum (arms, shoulders, hips, and free leg) but do not actually execute the turn. The result is that a minimal amount of active countermovement, so called "checking," is required to stop the rotation of the legs and feet. If you have ever had skating lessons or watched a practice at the local ice rink, you have probably heard the coach use the word "check." It is a very widely and often used but poorly defined word. When you have completed this step, you should understand the concept of checking and its importance and how individual checking can be.

Why Are Two-Foot Turns and Mohawks Important?

Two-foot directional changes include so-called "two-foot turns" and mohawks. In a two-foot turn, both feet remain on the ice during the change of direc-tion. With mohawks, although both feet are involved, only one foot is on the ice at a time. This is in contrast to three turns, which you'll learn later, in which directional changes are performed entirely on one foot. The main advantage of two-foot turns and the forward inside mohawk is that you can change direction from forward to backward at high and low speeds and without loss of speed. Two-foot turns are used commonly by hockey skaters and are a good preparation for mohawks. The forward inside mohawk is a much smoother way to change direction. It is often used as a transition from forward stroking to backward crossovers (Step 9). Figure skaters use its flow and controllability. It is also used as a transition from forward stroking to a backward glide in preparation for jumps. Variations of the forward inside mohawk are common elements of ice dancing.

Principle #5: "Turning Within Your Arms"

Similar to the fourth principle, in which your body box is prerotated to the inside of the curve being skated to help you stroke along the curve, your body box is also prerotated for the fifth principle. However, the purpose of your body box rotation is different. The fourth principle is used to help concentrate body weight and centrifugal forces directly onto the edge of the skate blade. The purpose of body box rotation in the fifth principle is to minimize and control rotational momentum caused by quickly turning your body from the forward to backward or backward to forward directions. When you are skating along a curve, your body box is always rotated to face toward the inside of the curve. In contrast, when you are turning, depending on the type of turn being executed, your body box may face into or out of the curve to control rotational momentum. Body box rotation is always toward the direction of the turn regardless if the turn is done with two feet, such as with two-foot turns and mohawks, or just one foot, as with three turns (Step 11). Setting and maintaining body box rotation before a turn insures that only your feet and legs have to "catch up" with the rest of your body during the turn with the result that rotational momentum is minimized.

In addition, your arms are extended and remain along the tracing or curve on which the turn is being executed to help with body box rotation and to eliminate any rotational momentum generated by moving them since they are furthest from the rotational axis of your body. Because your arms remain outstretched and unchanged throughout, turns appear to happen "within the arms."

The Concept of Body Axis

The concept of the vertical axis of rotation of your body in a turn is important to understand for balance and body control. If you are skating on two feet, this axis should run from your head down to the ice between your feet. If you are skating on one foot, the axis should run from your skating foot through your opposite shoulder. The purpose of setting the axis in these ways is to distribute your body mass equally around it.

When you change direction, such as in a three turn, your body box should rotate around this axis.

If your shoulders, arms, legs, or hips swing out too far from this axis, unnecessary rotational momentum is created (a wobble) that can throw you off balance. Once this momentum has been generated, it is very hard to control and must eventually be stopped. One way that this momentum is controlled is through "checking."

How to Execute Two-Foot Turns

Start the turn with a two-foot glide on a slight curve with your body box facing the inside of the circle (see Figure 8.1). Both knees are bent to support equal amounts of body weight. For a counterclockwise turn, slide your right foot in front of the left to an in-line position. Your left foot is on a slight outside edge and your right foot is on an inside edge. Your body weight is still supported by both legs. The back foot will turn backward onto an inside edge just a split second before your front foot turns onto a backward outside edge. You are now gliding backward with your feet still in a somewhat in-line position, left in front, right in back. Your body box is still facing the inside of the circle. If you place your feet next to each other again, the curve will straighten out and you'll be ready to skate backward using backward swizzles or stroking. Note, throughout the turn, your arms are aligned along the curve being skated and your body box is rotated to the center of the curve (turn within your arms, Principle #5).

FIGURE
8.1

KEYS TO SUCCESS

TWO-FOOT TURNS
Entrance to Turn

1. With speed, prerotate body box ___
2. Slide feet to in-line position ___
3. Place arms parallel to direction of travel ___

Turn and Exit From Turn

4. Turn back foot from forward to backward ___
5. Immediately, turn front foot from forward to backward ___
6. Turn is completed within your arms (no change in arm position) ___

How to Execute Forward Inside Mohawks

Mohawks are used to change skating direction from forward to backward or backward to forward. By definition, they involve a change of foot on a curve with edges of the same character. The forward inside mohawk begins with a forward inside edge on one foot and ends on a backward inside edge on your other foot. There are two methods to do mohawks, freestyle and dance. Though the movement is only slightly different and the results are virtually the same, they may look quite dissimilar. Both mohawks begin on a forward inside edge with your body box

rotated to face the inside of the curve being skated (see Figure 8.2a). During the approach to the turn, be sure the heel of the blade of your free foot does not cross behind the tracing. Your free leg is then brought heel first toward the instep of your skating foot (see Figure 8.2b and c). In the freestyle mohawk, both legs stay in a bent knee position throughout the maneuver. The knee bend accomplishes two things. First, it allows the skater to place the skate at a larger distance from the forward skating foot. Second, it makes the placing of the backward skating foot on the ice a lot easier. It does not require as much of a "turn out" of the leg.

For the dance mohawk, your skating leg is straightened as the heel of your free leg approaches the instep of your skating foot. The actual change of foot and weight transfer is completed on extended (straightened) knees.

With both mohawks, the approach of your free-leg foot to the instep of your skating foot is done by slightly lifting the corner of your body box on the free-leg side (see Figure 8.2b). Your free-leg knee stays in an open, turned-out position. It is crucial that the backward skating foot is placed on the ice on an in-

side edge and slightly to the inside of the curve (see Figure 8.2c and that figure's inset). The actual weight transfer is done smoothly by tilting your body box onto your new skating foot (see Figure 8.2d). Consistent with the light switch principle, the two skates should not be on the ice at the same time during a mohawk. The extension of the free leg after the mohawk is purely a choice of the skater or, in some cases, the demands of the rules in ice dancing.

FIGURE 8.2

KEYS TO SUCCESS

FORWARD INSIDE MOHAWK
Entrance to Turn

1. Rotation of body box to inside of curve ___
2. Lean of body box throughout mohawk ___
3. Extended free leg kept to inside of curve ___

Change of Feet

4. Free foot turned out ___
5. Bring heel of free foot to instep of skating foot (see insert) ___
6. Place backward foot on ice to the inside of the curve on a definite inside edge ___
7. Simultaneously lift forward foot off the ice (light switch principle) ___

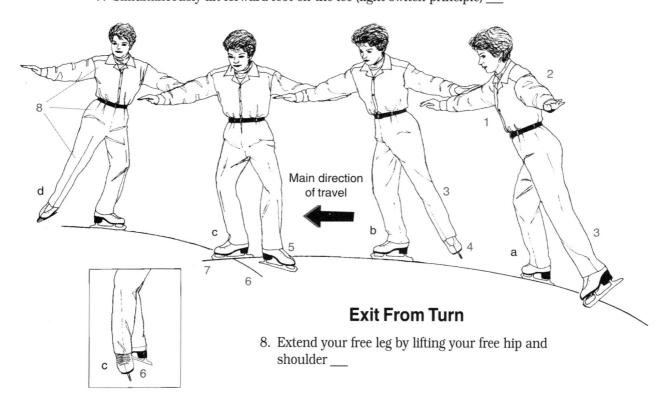

Main direction of travel

Exit From Turn

8. Extend your free leg by lifting your free hip and shoulder ___

TWO-FOOT TURNS AND MOHAWKS SUCCESS STOPPERS

One of the most important concepts in this step to remember is that your body is already prerotated at the time of the actual turn and change of direction. Therefore, the biggest success stopper is the insufficient prerotation in the direction of the turn (enough shoulder rotation but little or no hip rotation) and the lack of control of the rotational momentum that results.

Error	Correction
Two-Foot Turns	
1. You are curving but cannot complete the turn.	1. Your feet are side by side rather than in line. Move one foot and shoulder to the front in an in-line position.
2. You are able to turn, but your blades feel like they are "stuck."	2. You don't rotate your body box enough during the two-foot turn. Keep your shoulders and hips parallel with your direction of travel.
Forward Inside Mohawk	
1. You don't rotate your body box enough.	1. Beginners sometimes line up their arms parallel to the curve but fail to rotate their shoulders and hips. If you don't rotate your body box sufficiently, you won't be able to turn your backward foot out enough to place it on the ice for a smooth transition.
2. Your back foot strikes the ice to the outside of the curve.	2. You should place your back foot on the inside of the curve and on an inside edge.
3. You don't shift your weight from your forward to your back foot quickly enough.	3. Remember to execute the light switch principle. Review its components if necessary.
4. Your back foot skids when you place it on the ice.	4. Make sure that your forward foot is on a strong inside edge to give you a good curve and lean into the circle. This will allow you to place your back foot on an equally strong inside edge.
5. You switch your arms.	5. This creates undesired rotational momentum. Keep your arms extended along the line of travel.

TWO-FOOT TURNS AND MOHAWKS

DRILLS

1. Forward to Backward Two-Foot Turn

The purpose of this drill is to help you experience the principle of turning within your arms and at the same time teach you the basic methods for reversing direction. Start with a forward two-foot glide on a slight curve. Make sure that your body box faces the inside of the circle and that your arms extend along the curve.

For your turn, gradually let one foot slide ahead of the other. Keep your body weight on both feet. Let your back foot turn onto an inside edge just a split second before the front foot turns onto a backward outside edge. You'll end up in a backward two-foot glide with one foot still a bit in front of the other.

Success Goal = to reverse directions from forward to backward using a two-foot turn, both clockwise and counterclockwise ___

Success Check
- Body box remains facing the inside of the circle ___
- Arms are aligned along the curve being skated ___

To Increase Difficulty
- After your turn, bring your feet next to each other to skate along a straight path again. Use backward swizzles or stroking to increase your speed.
- Add a stop prior to repeating your two-foot turn in the opposite direction.

To Decrease Difficulty
- Try your two-foot turn(s) while facing the rink barrier by pushing off with one hand into a curve and catching yourself with the other hand on the barrier.

2. Two-Foot Turn With Step Forward

The main purpose of two-foot turns is to prepare you for mohawks; however, they can also be used to teach you how to step forward from backward glides. In fact, to practice two-foot turns, you can string several of them together by alternating the two-foot turn with a step forward. To step forward from a backward two-foot glide does not require a full 180-degree turn. A 90-degree turn to the side will be quite sufficient. For example, to step forward to your right, look to your right, turn your body box to your right, and pick up your right leg to prepare for the step. A slight turn out of your right foot close to your skating foot will enable you to step forward, transfer your weight onto your right foot and begin to travel forward. Use the light switch principle to transfer your weight completely to your right foot. Repeat on the opposite side.

Success Goal = to build speed with either forward swizzles or stroking, do a two-foot turn, and then step forward ___

Success Check
- Step forward on a 90-degree angle from skating curve ___
- Prior to your step, look to the new direction and rotate your body box ___

To Increase Difficulty
- In case of loss of speed during the two-foot turn, add speed with backward swizzles before the step forward.

3. Simulating Mohawks at the Rink Barrier

A simple, controlled method to get the feeling of the weight shift and lifting of your hips and shoulders in the light switch manner for the forward inside mohawk can be experienced at the rink barrier. When using the barrier, be sure you are at least an arm's length away from it in order to develop the necessary lean into the "curve" and also to give room for your back foot to be placed on an inside edge at the time of weight transfer. Practice mohawks at the barrier in both directions.

**Success Goal** = to change directions using a simulated mohawk at the rink barrier ___

Success Check

- Slightly lift and open the corner of your body box on your free-leg side toward the inside of the circle ___
- Place heel of free leg to instep of skating foot ___
- Shift weight onto the inside edge of your backward skating foot ___

4. Mohawks Away From the Barrier

Mohawks away from the barrier should be practiced in both directions. To confirm control of mohawks, check that the length and curvature of the arc of the entry edge are the same as the exit edge.

Success Goal = to change directions using a forward inside mohawk while away from the rink barrier ___

To Increase Difficulty

- Vary the amount of extension of your free leg after the mohawk.
- Use forward stroking to gain speed prior to your mohawk.

Success Check

- Only one skate is on the ice at a time ___

5. 180 Mohawk Sequence

While mohawks are often used to change direction, they can also be part of a repeating sequence and thus become "footwork." The 180 is more for the beginning skater who has just learned how to do a mohawk (see Figures 8.3a-c) and is not very confident about the backward inside edge at the completion of the maneuver (see Figure 8.3c). You can escape to a forward inside edge by merely stepping forward in the light switch fashion (see Figure 8.3d and e). From here you can take as many forward strokes as needed to get yourself reorganized to start this maneuver over. Or, the more advanced way would be to use the forward inside edge from the step forward as the start of the next mohawk.

Success Goal = to do the 180-degree mohawk sequence to both sides ___

Success Check
- Turn within your arms ___
- Alternately shift weight from one foot to the other ___

To Increase Difficulty
- String several mohawks in a row.

To Decrease Difficulty
- Perfect one side at a time.

Figure 8.3 The 180 mohawk sequence.

6. 360 Mohawk Sequence

For the 360, upon completion of the mohawk (see Figures 8.4a through d), continue backward on the same circle but switch to your other foot on a backward outside edge (see Figure 8.4e). Again your free-leg side is slightly lifted to insure that your body weight is directly over your skating foot and on the outside edge (see Figure 8.4f). From there, your objective is to step forward onto an outside edge on the same circle. This can only be accomplished by rotating your body box to face the outside of the circle (see Figure 8.4f). The most difficult part of this exercise is rotating your body from facing the inside of the circle to facing the outside. Often your upper body sags backward and makes the transition to the step forward very difficult since there is not enough weight over your skating foot. Your arms stay in relation to your body box and are moved along with that rotation. Before stepping forward, your free foot is brought to the heel of your skating foot (see Figure 8.4g). The step onto the forward outside edge should be a very small one in order to have your body weight shift smoothly with your sternum over your toes and to ensure continuous flow (see Figure 8.4h). If you desire to repeat this exercise, change your arms now before you step onto the forward inside edge to start the next mohawk. In performing a series of 360-degree turns, the most common error is failing to change from facing outside of the circle after stepping forward to facing inside the circle before starting the inside edge of the mohawk. This produces extra rotational momentum causing loss of control of the backward inside edge. Remember to switch your arms as close as possible to the skating axis (body) so as not to gain unwanted rotational momentum from your upper body.

Success Goal = to do the 360 mohawk sequence to both sides with a constant, nonhalting rhythm ___

Success Check

- Upon completion of the mohawk, switch to your other foot on a backward outside edge ___
- Alternately, your body box faces the inside of the circle, then the outside of the circle ___

To Increase Difficulty

- Perform a series of 360-degree sequences to both sides.

To Decrease Difficulty

- Practice each part separately.

Figure 8.4 The 360 mohawk sequence.

Main direction
of travel

TWO-FOOT TURNS AND MOHAWKS SUCCESS SUMMARY

In this step we've worked on turning within your arms, which decreases the rotational movement of large body parts such as your hips, shoulders, arms, and free leg during turns. By prerotating and holding the positions of your arms, shoulders, and hips, you'll reduce the need to forcibly check the movement of these body parts ("checking"). Although turning within your arms has been introduced in this step with the two-foot turn and mohawk, it can be applied to every other turn, as well.

Ask a trained observer to evaluate your progress with two-foot turns, mohawks, and steps forward using the checklists in Figures 8.1 and 8.2.

The Ice Skating Center in Davos, Switzerland. The massive outdoor rink in the foreground is complemented by an indoor rink in the intricately windowed building. Davos is the home of the International Skating Union and was visited often by the principal author of this book.

BACKWARD CROSSOVERS: GAINING SPEED ON A CURVE

L ike forward crossovers, backward crossovers are essential to gain speed on a curve. As in the forward crossover, we have a beginner version that allows you to learn the technique at a slower, more controlled speed. Eventually, you'll likely abandon the beginner version and use only the advanced backward crossovers, which generate much more speed with little extra work.

All of the major principles of ice skating—for example, keeping your body weight over your skating foot and prerotating and leaning your body box toward the inside of the curve you're skating—have been presented in the preceding steps. Now it's time to apply these principles to backward skating. You'll enjoy the exhilaration of speed and effortless gliding you can achieve while skating backward.

Why Are Backward Crossovers Important?

Backward crossovers are the most effective method to gain speed while skating backward on a curve. This is particularly true for advanced backward crossovers. They frequently precede spins, jumps, and other specialized skating maneuvers. In fact, there are usually more backward than forward crossovers in competitive and professional ice skating programs because of their efficiency and rapidity at gaining speed.

Backward Skateboard Pushes

Backward skateboard pushes can be used as a preparation for learning backward crossovers in the same way that you used forward skateboard pushes to learn forward crossovers. They will familiarize you with body box rotation and lean to the inside of the curve while skating backward on an outside edge. Begin by standing on two feet and turning your body box to face the inside of the curve to be skated (see Figure 9.1a). Keep your body weight steady over the outside edge of your gliding foot (the foot closer to the inside of the curve) and start making repeated pushes with your other foot. You'll get the feel of a backward outside edge that is very important for doing backward crossovers (Figure 9.1b).

Backward Glides

When you feel steady enough to glide on an outside edge in this one-foot position, practice extended backward glides with your free foot held forward and pigeon-toed across the tracing (see Figure 9.2). This skill brings you one step closer to doing the backward crossover, as this is the free-foot position that will allow you to place that foot on the ice on an inside edge in a crossed-foot position. Note that your body box is both rotated and tilted (medallion principle). Remember when skating on one foot that your body box must be tilted to ensure that your body weight is over your skating foot. The tilt of the skater shown in Figure 9.2 is apparent, as both her right hip and shoulder are higher than the left. Once you can do this, you're ready to do backward crossovers.

How to Execute Beginner Backward Crossovers

For the beginner backward crossover, keep both knees bent as you complete the maneuver. Throughout,

Figure 9.1 Backward skateboard push.

Figure 9.2 Backward outside edge glide with free foot pigeon-toed across the tracing.

your body box should be rotated to the center of the curve you're skating, with your arms extended over the tracing for balance and to help you judge that body box rotation has been achieved. Along with rotating your body box, lean your body toward the center of the curve. Following your initial push, your free foot is lifted pigeon-toed above the tracing (see Figure 9.3a). Note that your left (free) hip and shoulder are higher than your right to ensure that your body weight is over your skating foot.

Initiate the crossover by closing your thighs and lifting only your free foot over and across your skating foot from your knee down (Figure 9.3b). Your crossed free foot is still off the ice at this point. Now as the crossing foot makes contact with the ice on an inside edge, your body weight shifts instantly onto that foot (Figure 9.3c). The knee supporting your body weight remains bent. Briefly, you'll glide on two feet, with your crossing foot on an inside edge and your other foot on an outside edge. To uncross your feet, pick your back foot off the ice by lifting your knee upward and forward with the blade parallel to the ice (Figures 9.3d and e). Place your back foot on an outside edge next to your gliding foot in preparation for the next crossover (Figure 9.3f). As with all crossovers, your body weight shifts to the leg on the inside of the curve. Your head is rotated so that you can see into the direction of travel.

How to Execute Advanced Backward Crossovers

If you felt that you were working awfully hard for the amount of speed you were getting from beginner crossovers, you're right. The good news is that there is a way to gain more speed. The bad news is it is just as much work.

Similar to doing advanced forward crossovers, while performing the advanced backward crossover, you're best off forgetting the crossing-over process and concentrating on the crossing-*under*. In beginner backward crossovers, you picked up the foot on the outside of the curve and placed it over and to the side of your other foot. In advanced crossovers, your outside foot remains on the ice and glides on an inside edge while your other foot thrusts backward and under it (see Figure 9.4). This way you'll be able to develop a far deeper knee bend. You'll generate more

power and speed because the deeper your knee bend, the longer and more dynamic the leg thrusts with each push. With the advanced crossover, both legs contribute equally. As the blade of the foot on the inside of the curve makes contact with the ice, it is placed on an outside edge with all your body weight on it, just as in the beginner backward crossovers. The other foot, which remains on the ice and only supports the weight of that leg at this time, is on an inside edge at an angle determined by the degree of your knee bend. More knee bend means more inside edge. Apply pressure on the foot supporting your body weight on the inside of the curve and "shove" it under toward the outside of the curve to a full extension. This part of the crossover, which you have not yet practiced, will add a lot of speed.

Pretend you're in a dark rink with lights on your hands and head. The lights should remain level above the ice throughout, and no one should be able to detect the different stages of the crossover (i.e., no limping or up and down movements).

We'll summarize the most important features of the advanced backward crossover:

1. The foot on the outside of the curve remains on an inside edge, while the foot on the inside of the curve remains on an outside edge throughout (see Figure 9.4).
2. Keep the foot on the outside of the curve on the curve's circumference while thrusting your other foot toward the outside foot and behind it until the leg is fully extended (Figures 9.4a-e).
3. Your weight remains on the foot being thrust under and backward until both feet are in line; then all of your body weight shifts to the foot in front (Figures 9.4c and d).
4. Perform the last part of the crossunder without any body weight on the foot that is thrust under (Figures 9.4e and f).

The major speed gain occurs from when your inside foot contacts the ice (Figures 9.4a and h) to when your weight shifts and your feet are in line (between Figures 9.4c and d and between i and j). The contribution of the outside leg thrust to generating power and speed is the same as for the beginner crossover but is more forceful here because you bend your knees more and keep your skate on the ice, making the push longer (Figures 9.4f and g).

FIGURE
9.3

KEYS TO SUCCESS

BEGINNER BACKWARD CROSSOVERS

Backward Outside Glide

1. Body box rotation and lean to inside of curve ___
2. Free foot pigeon-toed and suspended above tracing ___

Crossover and Weight Shift

3. Thighs closed ___
4. Free foot crossed to inside of curve ___
5. Weight shifts to foot on inside of curve on an inside edge ___

Retrieval of Back Foot

6. Retrieve back foot by lifting your knee upward and forward ___
7. Keep thighs closed ___

Weight Transfer

8. Place retrieved foot on an outside edge ___

Crossover

9. Repeat keys 1 through 8 ___

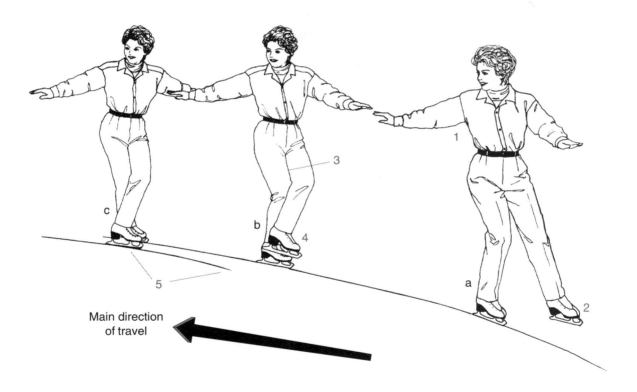

Main direction
of travel

FIGURE
9.4 **KEYS TO SUCCESS**

ADVANCED BACKWARD CROSSOVERS

Step to Inside of Curve With Weight Transfer

1. Body box rotation and lean to inside of curve ___
2. Outside foot on a constant inside edge ___
3. Inside leg supports weight ___
4. Inside foot placed on outside edge ___
5. Inside knee is bent ___

Inside Leg Crossunder and Thrust

6. Thrust inside foot under ___
7. Shift weight to front foot as thrusting foot passes behind it ___

Retrieval of Inside Leg and Outside Leg Thrust Phase

8. Retrieve your free leg to the point of uncrossing ___
9. Increase pressure on inside edge of skating foot and thrust ___

Repeat of Step to Inside of Curve

10. Shift weight totally to inside foot ___
11. Repeat ___

Main direction
of travel

BACKWARD CROSSOVERS SUCCESS STOPPERS

The errors for beginner and advanced backward crossovers are essentially the same. Of course, with the potential for speed gain with the advanced version, problems have a tendency to become compounded; it is, therefore, best to familiarize yourself thoroughly with the success stoppers.

Error	Correction
1. You don't bend your knees enough. This is often signaled by blades clinking together, tripping, lack of power, or an irregular, limping appearance.	1. When one leg is supporting your weight, bend the knee of that leg. When you're shifting weight, bend both knees.
2. You don't gain speed and there is a lot of scratching with each crossover.	2. The scratching is caused by the toepick, usually on the foot that crosses under, when too much weight remains on it. You don't transfer your weight completely.
3. You have difficulty shifting your weight, you feel a loss of balance, and your crossovers are unsteady and give a limping appearance.	3. These common errors result from rocking and twisting your upper body. Keep your body box facing and leaning into the curve you're skating. Keep your arms extended along the curve to help keep your balance (but this will not in itself prevent twisting motions).

BACKWARD CROSSOVERS

DRILLS

1. Backward Skateboard Pushes

Start with a two-foot backward glide and turn your body box to face the inside of the curve to be skated. Let your body weight transfer to the outside edge of the foot closest to the inside of the curve, which becomes your gliding foot. Make repeated pushes with your other foot to maintain your speed. If you are not yet comfortable gliding backward on an outside or inside edge, it is probably a good idea that you continue to practice backward skateboard pushes to both sides until you feel comfortable.

Success Goal = to become comfortable doing one-foot backward glides on an outside edge ___

Success Check
• Prerotate your body box to face the inside of the curve ___
• Push with the inside edge of your outside foot ___

To Increase Difficulty
• Lengthen the time that you glide backward on an outside edge, using either foot.

To Decrease Difficulty
• Shorten the time that you glide backward on an outside edge.

2. Long Backward Edge Glides

When you're doing one-foot backward glides on an outside edge, test your stability and balance for backward crossovers by practicing long one-foot glides on an inside edge. Again, practice on both sides.

Success Goal = to hold an outside or inside edge for a distance equal at least to your height ___

Success Check
• Keep thighs closed ___
• Free foot is pigeon-toed and suspended above the tracing ___

3. Beginner Backward Crossovers

Beginner backward crossovers prepare you for advanced crossovers. From a backward glide on an outside edge, lift and cross your free foot over your gliding foot. When your crossing foot contacts the ice on an inside edge, let your body weight transfer onto that foot. Briefly glide on two feet. To uncross your feet, lift the knee of your back foot and bring it forward with the blade parallel to the ice. Make sure you retrieve your crossed foot without scratching the ice with your toepick. This should be done without loss of speed and to both sides.

Success Goal = to comfortably execute beginner backward crossovers ___

Success Check
• Prerotate your body box ___
• Lean toward the inside of the curve ___
• Arms extended over the tracing for balance ___
• Keep both knees bent ___
• Transfer weight from an outside to an inside edge ___

To Increase Difficulty
• Alternately do beginner backward crossovers to one side, then to the other.
• Make a figure-8 path on the ice.

4. Advanced Backward Crossovers

Your outside foot remains on the ice and glides on an inside edge while the other foot thrusts backward and under it (review Figure 9.4, pp. 104-105). You'll need to deepen your knee bend throughout, which will give each leg thrust more power. The blade of your outside leg remains on an inside edge throughout and close to the circumference of the arc of the circle being skated, even when your inside foot crosses under. Practice on both sides.

Success Goal =
a. to keep in and out oscillations of your outside foot to a minimum ___
b. to generate an equal amount of speed with both thrusts ___

Success Check
• Both legs bent throughout ___
• Both legs contribute equally ___

5. Two-Foot Change of Direction

At the completion of a crossunder in one direction (see Figure 9.5a), retrieve the crossed-under foot (Figure 9.5b) and place it on the ice as if you were continuing with another crossunder (Figure 9.5c). Don't do the crossunder, but keep your feet separated by this large distance. Shift your body weight to your other leg, which squares your body box temporarily to the skating direction (Figures 9.5d and e). Turn your head and body box into the new direction and continue with crossovers (Figure 9.5f).

Success Goal = to change direction without loss of speed and without rising out of the knee bend ___

Success Check
• Keep weight on both feet ___
• Rotate your body box toward the inside of each curve ___

To Increase Difficulty
• Vary the number of crossovers between each change of direction and cover as much of the rink as possible.

Figure 9.5 Two-foot change of direction during backward crossovers.

6. *Change of Direction With a One-Foot Backward Outside Glide*

This drill is commonly used during warm-ups and involves a one-foot glide on a backward outside edge and a transitional body box rotation into the new direction. At the completion of the last backward crossover in one direction, retrieve your crossed-under leg (see Figure 9.6a) and place it on a backward outside edge with your body box still facing the inside of the curve (Figure 9.6b). Simultaneously, lift your other foot (the outside foot) off the ice and extend it fully to the back. Drop your arms to the sides of your body and rotate your head and body box to the outside of the curve (Figures 9.6c and d). With the lifting of your arms and full extension of your free leg over the tracing, you're still on an outside edge and on the original curve (Figure 9.6e). Bring your free foot back to the level of your gliding foot and to the inside of the new curve without touching the ice and while keeping both knees bent (Figure 9.6f). Because of your body box rotation and the weight of your free foot, the skating edge will switch from outside to inside. You're now ready to step onto an outside edge with your free foot and proceed with crossovers in the new direction (Figures 9.6g and h).

Success Goal = to have generated enough speed in the crossovers to produce a steady controlled backward outside glide that enables you to rotate your body box to continue crossovers in the new direction ___

To Increase Difficulty

• Make continuous figure-8s that cover as much of the rink as possible.

Success Check

• Arms come to sides as head and body box rotate to face the inside of the new curve ___
• Skating edge switches from outside to inside ___

7. *Connect Backward Crossovers With Forward Crossovers and Mohawks*

Finally, there is a drill which incorporates advanced forward crossovers, inside mohawks, advanced backward crossovers, and a step to forward.

Begin with three forward crossovers in the counterclockwise direction. As the third crossover ends on a right forward inside edge, this edge now becomes the entry edge of a right inside mohawk. Retrieve your left foot from its crossed-under position, turn your left foot out, and bring your left heel to the instep of your right foot. Perform the mohawk. Place your right leg on a backward outside edge to the inside of the curve and begin three backward advanced counterclockwise crossovers. At the end of the third backward crossover, you're skating on a left backward inside edge. Retrieve your right foot from its crossed-under position and turn it out. Step forward toward the inside of the curve onto a right inside edge (see Figures 8.3d and e, p. 94). Start counterclockwise forward crossovers again and repeat the sequence. Note that this sequence continues around the same counterclockwise curve, but it should also be done in the clockwise direction.

Success Goal = to maintain a continuous rhythm throughout the sequence ___

Success Check

• Unchanged prerotation and lean of your body box into the curve ___
• Maintain a constant knee bend ___
• Rotate within your arms ___

To Increase Difficulty

• Add style by fully extending your free leg as it leaves the ice.

To Decrease Difficulty

• Gradually add each part of the sequence.

Figure 9.6 One-foot backward outside glide change of direction sequence for backward crossovers.

BACKWARD CROSSOVERS SUCCESS SUMMARY

Backward crossovers share with forward crossovers body box rotation and lean to generate power for gaining and maintaining speed while skating on a curve. It is the combination of body box rotation and lean that helps concentrate centrifugal and body weight forces onto the skate blades. Successful execution of backward crossovers doubles the pleasure of skating in several ways. Suddenly, your skating becomes multidimensional. The possibilities of changing directions from side to side and from forward to backward and backward to forward in any sequence and in combination with speed can give you a natural high. Ask a trained observer to evaluate your performance using the checklists in Figures 9.3 and 9.4. Note the similarities to the checklists for forward crossovers.

Pond at a maple sugar shack on Irish Settlement Road, Underhill, Vermont, with Mount Mansfield in the background.

STEP
10

SWINGROLLS AND ADVANCED EDGES:
IMPROVING EDGE CONTROL

Controlling inside and outside edges while gliding forward or backward is truly the cornerstone of all forms of ice skating. Traditionally, edges *were* figure skating. The old masters proved their proficiency of ice skating by drawing complicated patterns on the ice using different edges and turns. To this day, there are two individuals considered the best at this art: Gillis Grafström of Sweden, who was the men's Olympic champion in 1920, 1923, and 1928, and Beatrix "Trixi" Schuba of Austria, who was the women's Olympic champion in 1972. Although complex figures are not required in competition today, many noncompetitors as well as competitors still enjoy them because they are the one area of ice skating where you can see yourself clearly approach perfection.

The importance of edges of course goes beyond creating graphics on ice. You cannot progress beyond a very basic level without command of edges. Not only are they necessary for many skating moves (such as *three turns*, which we'll introduce in Step 11), they also greatly improve skills you've already learned, including forward and backward crossovers and mohawks. Edge control has been a key element to the success of champion figure skaters from Sonja Henie to Brian Boitano, the ice hockey superstars such as Gordie Howe and Wayne Gretsky, and the powerful speedskaters Dan Jansen and Bonnie Blair. If you get the chance, watch one of Sonja Henie's old movies. While her figure skating style might be considered archaic today, her edges are deep and strong.

Our goal in this step is to develop more control of inside and outside edges in both the forward and backward directions. We'll introduce two categories of edge control: *Advanced edges*, designed to skate

half- and full circles, are the standard, time-proven method to learn edges taught by most instructors, whereas *swingrolls* are designed to form sweeping curves used primarily in ice dancing. If you believed you had mastered your body box and skating posture concepts in the previous steps, wait until you try controlling edges. More than anything you have experienced so far, advanced edges and swingrolls will demand precise control and understanding of the five skating principles.

Why Are Swingrolls and Advanced Edges Important?

The precise control of edges to skate a perfect circle, half-circle, or turn is only one aspect of why you should strive to learn them. Ice dancing demands control and precision of edges, not unlike figures, and is complicated by the addition of a partner and music. The modern champions of competitive freestyle ice skating have a supreme command of edges, allowing them to jump higher, land more securely, and spin faster than their predecessors. Even for recreational skaters, especially those who want to do advanced maneuvers or ice dance, edge control is paramount. An uncontrolled edge that skids on an entry to a jump or a spin usually produces weak results at best. A poorly controlled edge on an exit from a jump can be painful and is the basis for the phrase, "Seek the safety of the edge when exiting a jump." But control of edges is not only limited to figure skaters. Adept hockey players also have command of the edges, which allows them to change direction, reverse direction, and stop instantaneously.

How to Execute Forward Swingrolls

We'll begin edge control with swingrolls because they are usually easier than advanced edges. In swingrolls, your arms remain in the same position from beginning to end, square to the main direction of travel. In other words, all of your curving is done "within the arms." The swingroll is a dance term, and although the maneuver is primarily used in dancing, most recreational skaters also enjoy doing it. The word *swingroll* almost explains itself. The "swing" relates to your free leg, which is swung from full backward extension to the front or the back depending on whether you are moving forward or backward. The "roll" relates to the pattern on the ice, which consists of long sweeping curves somewhat like rolling hills. As a rule, you want to reduce upper body rotation as much as possible. Achieve this by leaving your arms extended at hip to waist level at a place where you still see both of your hands out of the corners of your eyes. The rotation occurs with your body box inside your arms and your chin in line with your sternum (centered over your body box).

Forward Outside Swingroll

When you start your first outside swingroll, you'll face one hand and, at the end, before you start the next outside swingroll, you should be facing the other hand. The push is like a thrust to an outside edge or a skateboard push with your body box facing the inside of the prospective circle (see Figures 10.1a and e, pp. 116-117). Upon extension of your free leg to the back (Figure 10.1f), rise from your skating-leg knee bend and gently "swing" your free leg to the front (Figures 10.1b-d and g-i). Make sure that the passage of your free leg is in a straight line and very close to your skating foot. Your free hip stays up to ensure that your body weight remains solidly over your outside edge (body box tilted and undistorted). Once your free leg is extended to the front, point your toe, slightly pigeon-toed, in the direction of the curve, and hold onto that position (Figures 10.1d and i). The minimum diameter of your curves should be at least equal to your height. Before you can push for the next swingroll to the opposite side, you'll have to bend your knees (Figure 10.1e). Then bring your free foot back from the forward extension next to your skating foot, but keep it off the ice. Bend both knees, push, and shift your body weight in a light switch fashion, as described earlier. Your new curve starts parallel to the end of the old curve.

At the end of your swingroll there may be moderate distortion of your body box when your free leg is fully extended to the front (see Figures 10.1d and i). The degree of distortion depends on how far forward your leg extends and how high you lift your arms. In this case, the counterrotation of your shoulders relative to the direction of the curve you're skating counteracts the tendency for overrotation caused by your free-leg foot being brought forward. Keep distortion to a minimum, but it is a result of the maneuver and is a part of the good feeling inherent in swingrolls. The distortion also produces a diagonal tension in your body box, which prepares you to start the next half-circle in a new direction. The style aspect of the swingroll is clear in Figure 10.1, with the skater's arms and shoulders maintained mostly square to the main direction of travel and the free leg forward.

FIGURE
10.1

KEYS TO SUCCESS

FORWARD OUTSIDE SWINGROLL

(see pp. 116-117)

Initial Push

1. At the push, face the arm opposite the skating leg ___
2. At start of glide, tilt body box ___

The Leg Swing

3. Rise out of skating knee bend ___
4. Pass free leg close to skating leg ___
5. Keep free foot pigeon-toed over tracing ___
6. Hold position as required by music or count ___
7. Minimize body box distortion ___

Transition Push

8. Bring feet together ___
9. Bend both knees ___
10. Remain gliding on one foot and push to new direction (light switch) ___

Consecutive Forward Outside Swingrolls

11. Arms remain extended and square to the main direction of travel ___
12. Turn within your arms ___
13. Head remains in line with your sternum and skating foot ___

Figure 10.1 Forward outside swingroll.

Forward Inside Swingroll

The forward inside swingroll is similar to its forward outside counterpart—the one difference is that it's performed on an inside edge. The initial push is like forward inside stroking, where the foot of your skating leg is in line under your armpit (see Figures 10.2a and e). Don't let the heel of your free foot cross behind the tracing of your skating foot after the push, as this can pull your free hip down. Again, you rise from the knee bend of your skating leg before you bring your free leg forward (see Figures 10.2b and f) while passing it as close as possible to your skating foot (Figures 10.2c and g). Since the lean of your body is to the inside of the curve, you must bend your free leg as you bring it forward to prevent the free skate blade from contacting the ice. Once your free leg is fully extended to the front (Figure 10.2d), do not try to turn out your free foot too much, as that usually encourages your free hip to drop and your edge to collapse. Keep your arms extended perpendicular to your primary skating direction (side to side); your body box rotates inside your arms, with your sternum over your skating foot. To progress to the next push, bend both knees, keeping your free foot off the ice until after the push to the opposite side (Figures 10.2h and i).

How to Execute Backward Swingrolls

Backward swingrolls, outside or inside, can be quite challenging. Your backward skating needs to be fairly strong with good balance and control. Start your swingrolls with some speed from either backward crossovers or backward stroking. Extend your arms side to side at hip to armpit level. As long as your arms stay between your hips and your armpits, they can be considered correct—however, the lower they are, the easier they are controlled. (The higher they are, the more they can cause swinging of your body box.) Your body box rotates inside the arms.

Backward Outside Swingroll

Backward swingrolls share many similarities with forward swingrolls. The most obvious is that your arms and shoulders remain square to the main direction of travel (see Figure 10.3). To begin the backward outside swingroll to the right (counterclockwise), push with your left leg onto a right backward outside edge while facing your right arm (Figures 10.3a-c). Do the pushes as described for backward stroking and beginner crossovers with your free foot slightly pigeon-toed over the tracing and extended to the front. Your free hip is up to ensure that your body weight is directly over the outside edge of your skating foot. Other similarities to the forward swingroll are the straightening of the knee of the skating leg after the push and the close proximity of your passing free leg to your skating leg (Figures 10.3d, e, and i-k). At the full extension of your free leg to the back (Figures 10.3f and l), your body box is slightly distorted, which gives the swingroll its stylish character. Keep the distortion to a minimum by not letting the heel of your free leg blade cross the tracing. As with all backward outside pushes, your thighs should remain squeezed together from the push onto the backward outside edge and until your free leg passes your skating leg (Figures 10.3a-d and g-j).

Unlike forward swingrolls, where your head, sternum, and skating toes are in line, here your head is turned backward in the direction of travel. A big difference between backward crossovers and backward outside swingrolls is that in crossovers your body box faces the inside of the circle constantly and, for backward outside swingrolls, your body box faces the outside of the curve initially and faces the inside at the end. This is why these edges are so tricky. They might feel awkward because your back is facing the inside of the circle, giving you the feeling that you'll fall backward. Once you get over the natural apprehension of turning your back to the circle, you're on the way to a great backward swingroll.

Backward Inside Swingroll

Your back remains facing the main direction of travel with backward inside swingrolls, just as in backward outside swingrolls. With each push, your head looks over your skating-foot shoulder (see Figures 10.4a and d). But unlike backward outside swingrolls, where your head turns at the very end of the curve just before the push into the new direction, here your head turns along with the passage of your free leg about midway through the curve (Figures 10.4b, e, f). With the full extension of your free leg and turn of your head, you continue skating to the end of that curve (Figures 10.4c and g). As on all inside edges, your free-leg hip is not lifted and, therefore, your free leg must bend as it passes from front to back (Figure 10.4b).

FIGURE 10.2

KEYS TO SUCCESS

FORWARD INSIDE SWINGROLL

Initial Push

1. At the push, face the arm of your skating leg ___
2. At start of glide, tilt body box ___

The Leg Swing

3. Rise out of skating knee bend ___
4. Pass free leg close to skating leg by bending its knee ___
5. Keep free foot blade parallel to the ice and over the tracing ___
6. Hold position as required by music or count ___
7. Minimize body box distortion ___

Transition Push

8. Bring feet together ___
9. Bend both knees ___
10. Remain gliding on one foot until end of push (light switch) ___

Consecutive Forward Inside Swingrolls

11. Arms remain extended and square to the main direction of travel ___

12. Turn within your arms ___
13. Head remains in line with your sternum and skating foot ___

FIGURE
10.3

KEYS TO SUCCESS

BACKWARD OUTSIDE SWINGROLL

Initial Push

1. Body box faces to the inside of the curve ___
2. Keep thighs closed after push ___
3. Keep free-leg foot pigeon-toed over tracing ___

The Leg Swing

4. Arise from knee bend ___
5. Pass free leg close to skating leg ___

Transition Push

6. Bend both knees ___
7. Bring feet together while remaining on one foot ___
8. Turn head to new curve to be skated ___
9. Repeat to other direction ___

Main direction of travel

**FIGURE
10.4** **KEYS TO SUCCESS**

BACKWARD INSIDE SWINGROLL

Initial Push

1. Body box faces away to the outside of the curve ___
2. Thighs closed ___
3. Free-leg foot pigeon-toed and over the tracing ___

The Leg Swing

4. Head turns as free leg is bent and passes close to skating leg ___
5. Extend free leg fully to back ___
6. Free foot heel over tracing ___
7. Complete body box rotation to face the inside of the curve within your arms ___

Transition Push

8. Bend both knees ___
9. Repeat push and curve to other side ___

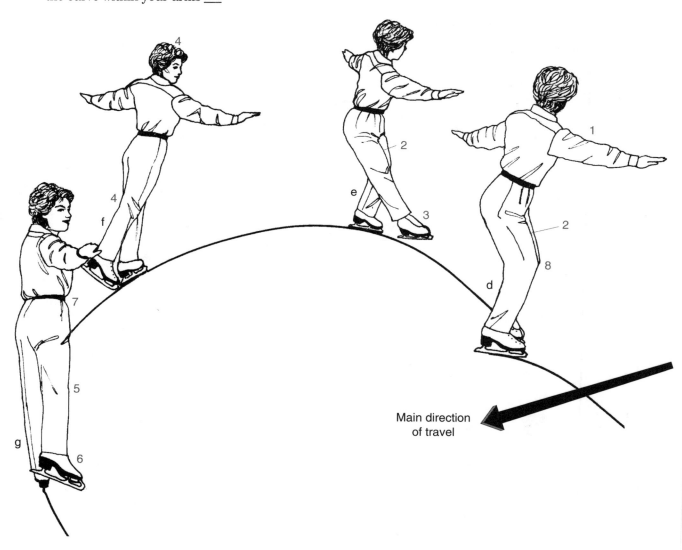

Main direction of travel

How to Execute Advanced Edges

Much of the control you learned for swingrolls will help you master advanced edges. Done correctly, advanced edges can be extended to full circles, such as in figures, or even to spirals (see below). Consecutive half-circles from a standstill on forward and backward and inside and outside edges are commonly required in skating tests. For the latter, the half-circles must be of equal size with a radius about equal to the skater's height. There is a long axis in the main direction of travel, and the semicircles are to each side of that axis. True semicircles are generally required. Regardless of the type of advanced edge, the pushes are made perpendicular to and begin on the long axis.

Spirals get their name from the pattern carved into the ice when a forward or backward edge is held unchanged for a long time and the slowing speed causes the radius of the curve to steadily decrease. Spirals are usually done with your body bent forward at the waist and your free leg extended backward with your foot up higher than your head. The strength and edge control required to do spirals have made them a favorite maneuver of both men and women skaters. Spirals give the illusion of flying across the ice.

Advanced Forward Outside Edges

For advanced forward edges, begin from a standstill in the T-position. To begin with a left forward outside edge, form a T-position by placing the heel of your left foot at the instep of your right foot (your two feet are at right angles to each other; see Figure 10.5a). Your arms extend over the toes of their respective feet; your left arm is forward over your left toes and your right arm slightly to the side and backward over your right toes. The center of your sternum is over your left toes. Push vigorously enough to gain the speed necessary to complete a half-circle on the forward outside edge (Figure 10.5b). Note that your skating knee is bent and your sternum is directly over your left toes. Rise to a straight leg (Figure 10.5c). At this time in swingrolls, you moved your free leg forward in a continuous motion from full back extension to full forward extension, the swinging of your free leg producing controlled rotational momentum, which resulted in an oval rather than a circular curve. With advanced edges, your goal is to avoid any extraneous rotational momentum so that a true semi- or full circle can be skated. As your free leg passes forward, bring it to rest with your toe at the heel of your skating foot (Figures 10.5c and d). At first, your free knee still points in a 90-degree angle outward. After your free toe contacts your skating heel, close your thighs and point your free knee forward (Figure 10.5d). Notice that the right side of your body box is elevated (Principle #1—body weight over skate). This is the "freeze it" position you can use if you want to continue gliding on a complete circle or further into a spiral.

The next sequence of moves is designed to prepare you to step into the new direction. They are done in two stages. First, your free leg extends to the front, with your free foot pigeon-toed across the tracing (Figure 10.5e). The lower part of your body is now ready for the next push, but the upper isn't. You must now bring your arms down and next to your body to prevent creating rotational momentum (Figures 10.5f and g) and then lift them into the switched position (Figure 10.5h). You can now perform the push into the new direction (Figures 10.5i-k). Because you are on an outside edge, and since pushes on one foot are performed with an inside edge, you might be wondering how the edge change occurs. As you bring your free foot back to your skating foot from its forward extension and bend both knees in anticipation of the push, the skating blade will automatically roll over onto its inside edge, and the trace will bend toward the inside of the circle for the push (Figure 10.5i). This push again uses the light switch technique (see Figure 6.1, p. 64).

FIGURE
10.5

KEYS TO SUCCESS

ADVANCED FORWARD OUTSIDE EDGES

Initial Setup

1. T-position with future gliding blade 90 degrees to long axis ___

The Initial Push

2. Strong push to forward outside edge ___
3. Sternum over skating toes ___
4. Lift free side of body box ___
5. Straighten skating knee ___
6. Bring free foot toe to heel of skating foot ___

Free Leg Extension

7. Close thighs ___
8. Extend free leg forward ___
9. Pigeon-toe free foot over tracing ___

Arm Switch

10. Switch arm position close to body ___

Transition Push

11. Bring free foot back to skating foot ___
12. Bend knees in preparation for next push ___

Advanced Forward Inside Edges

Advanced forward inside edges are best begun in the T-position with your arms framing your front foot and your sternum centered over its toes (see Figure 10.6a). Push onto an inside edge with a bent knee (Figure 10.6b). Rise out of your knee bend and bring your free foot toe to the heel of your skating foot for the same reasons this was done with advanced forward outside edges (Figure 10.6c). Since your body lean is always toward the inside of the circle, your free hip (the inside hip) will not be lifted—rather, both hips should remain parallel to the surface of the ice. This again is the "freeze it" position, which allows you to continue to a full circle or beyond. The following moves prepare you for a change in direction onto the other foot to the opposite side. Again they are done in stages: The free foot moves to the front (Figures 10.6d-f), then your arms are switched close to your body (Figures 10.6e-g and g*) and your knees are bent in preparation for the push (Figures 10.6i and i*). Because you are on an inside edge, increasing the angle of the blade on that inside edge will cause the tracing to deviate out of the circle you have been skating (Figure 10.6i*). You are now ready to push in the light switch manner (Figures 10.6i*, i-l).

Advanced Backward Outside Edges

Like forward outside edges, backward outside edges can be used to glide for a full circle or long spirals. Consecutive semicircular backward outside edges are often encountered in test situations; however, this is not their main function. They are necessary for many maneuvers such as approaches to spins and jumps and changing directions in backward crossovers.

Begin by standing at the top of and facing down the long axis to be skated. Start the initial push by bending your knees, shifting your weight onto your pushing foot, and thrusting onto a backward outside edge (see Figures 10.7a-c). Your body box faces and leans into the circle (remember Principle #4—the medallion principle; see Figures 10.7a-e). Your arms are extended over the tracing. After the push, your free leg is in front, with your free foot pigeon-toed (Figures 10.7c and k). You now rise from your skating-foot knee-bend, and slowly bring your free foot to the heel of your skating foot by bending your leg only from your knee downward and keeping your thighs together as close as possible (Figures 10.7d, e, l, and m). Your free toe should not pass beyond the heel of your skating foot. Your free knee should still be pointing over your past tracing in the same direction as your skating knee. This is the "freeze it" position if you wish to continue skating a full circle or beyond. To prepare for the push into the new direction, switch your arms and rotate your body box, which you do by lowering your arms to your sides (Figure 10.7f), turning your body box and your head to face the outside of the circle (Figure 10.7g), and lifting your arms in the "switched" position (Figures 10.7h and i). Throughout, keep your free hip up to ensure an outside edge and your body weight over your skating foot (skating axis through skating foot and opposite shoulder). By bending your skating knee and increasing the pressure on your blade, the edge will change from outside to inside as you come into a perfect position to push into the semicircle to the other side (Figure 10.7j). With a clean transfer of weight, your left foot is placed on a backward outside edge and the process is repeated (Figures 10.7k-m).

FIGURE
10.6

KEYS TO SUCCESS

ADVANCED FORWARD INSIDE EDGES

Initial Setup

1. T-position with the future gliding blade 90 degrees to the long axis (arms are about 90 degrees apart and frame your gliding foot) ___
2. Bend knees ___

Initial Push

3. Strong push to inside edge ___
4. Sternum over toes ___
5. Rise out of knee bend ___
6. Bring free-foot toe to heel of skating foot with knee pointing outward ___

Free Leg Extension

7. Bring free foot forward over tracing ___

Arm Switch

8. Switch arms close to body ___

Transition Push

9. Bring your free foot back ___
10. Bend both knees ___
11. Strong push into next circular curve ___

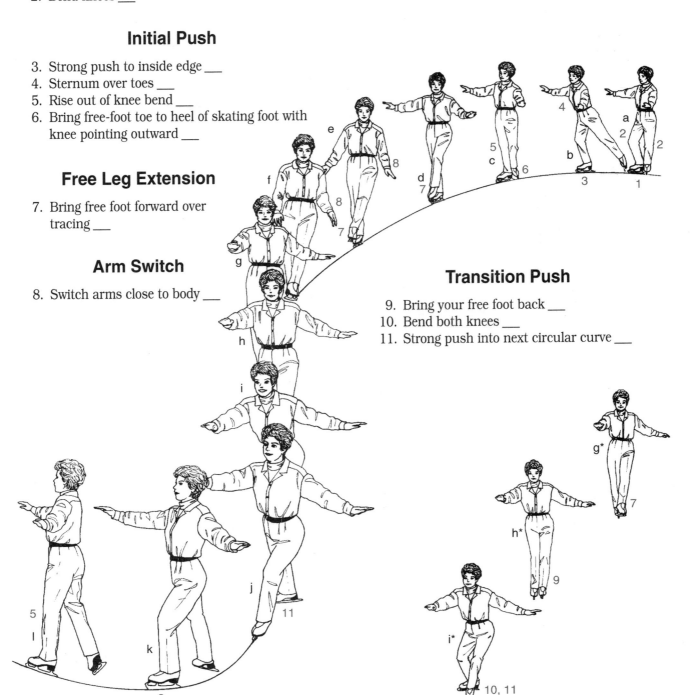

FIGURE
10.7

KEYS TO SUCCESS

ADVANCED BACKWARD OUTSIDE EDGES

Initial Push

1. Face the main axis of travel ___
2. Strong push to a back outside edge ___
3. Body box faces inside of semicircle ___
4. Close thighs and pigeon-toe free foot over tracing ___
5. Extend arms over tracing ___

Final Positioning of Free Leg

6. Rise from skating knee bend ___
7. Bring free-foot toe to heel of skating foot ___

Arm Switch and Body Rotation

8. Lower arms to sides of body ___
9. Begin body box rotation to outside of semicircle ___
10. Turn head to outside of semicircle ___
11. Continue body box rotation to outside of semicircle ___
12. Raise arms to waist level in "switched" position ___
13. Complete body box rotation ___

Transition Push

14. Bring free foot next to skating foot ___
15. Bend both knees in preparation for the push in new direction ___
16. Push onto the opposite back outside edge and repeat ___

Advanced Backward Inside Edges

Backward inside edges seem easier for a lot of skaters because less movement is required to rotate your body box, its rotation is much more subtle, and subsequent pushes are similar to backward stroking pushes. However, the initial push from a standstill tends to be more challenging, so we feel compelled to describe it separately and in more detail (see Figure 10.8).

For the initial push to advanced backward inside edges, begin by facing away from the long skating axis (Figure 10.8a). For a push to a back right inside edge, place all of your weight on your pushing foot, left (Figures 10.8a and b). Both knees are bent and your free foot, right, is suspended very closely to your skating foot and just barely above the ice. Your left arm is extended to your side, and your right arm is crossed in front of your body to help with balance and to help generate momentum at the time of the push. As you transfer your weight onto the backward inside edge of your skating foot, your right arm extends over the tracing, and your pushing foot comes off the ice and becomes your free foot (Figure 10.8c). The preparatory countermotion followed by lateral extension of the future gliding foot and arm are done in one continuous motion. Although your thighs separate for the actual weight transfer, they are brought together immediately to ensure that your free leg remains over the tracing and your body weight is securely over your inside edge (Figures 10.8c and d). Your skating knee is straightened (Figures 10.8e and f). This push to a backward inside edge is the same regardless of the intended maneuver. At this point (Figure 10.8f), you can enter a swingroll or any other maneuver on a backward inside edge.

Following the initial push from a standstill, make sure to strike a solid inside edge with your skating foot by balancing your weight directly over that edge (see Figures 10.9a-c). Immediately after the push, your pushing leg becomes a free leg and is extended to the front with your thighs close together and your free foot pigeon-toed over the tracing. Now it is time to rise from your skating-knee bend, bring the toe of your free foot to the heel of your skating foot and simultaneously turn your head to the inside of the circle (Figures 10.9d and e). To prevent excess rotation of your buttocks, bend your free leg only from your knee downward and keep that knee pointing to the front. At this point you have skated approximately a quarter of a circle. Your position facing the outside of the circle and your arm position during the first quarter circle were to compensate for the push. In the next quarter, you reorganize the position of your body box, your arms, and your free leg for either continuous gliding on a backward inside edge or a push into the opposite direction. Note that in the first quarter (Figures 10.9a-e), your body box faces to the outside of the circle. Your body box has to face to the inside of the circle and the arms have to be switched in order to get to the "freeze it" position in contrast to backward outside edges where the "freeze it" position occurred before body box rotation. One of the challenges of backward inside edges is to coordinate body box rotation, the passage of your free leg to its backward position, and switching arms. All of this should be completed at the same time (Figures 10.9f-h). This is the "freeze it" position (h) and may be held for an extended period. If you had intended to hold this edge for longer than a half circle, we suggest that your free-leg toe be brought to the heel of your skating foot. To push into the opposite direction, bring your free leg next to your skating leg by bending both knees (Figure 10.9i). The push is essentially the same as from a standstill explained earlier (Figure 10.8) except that you don't have to create momentum by counter movements of your arm and leg (Figures 10.9j-p).

Figure 10.8 Push from a standstill to a backward inside edge.

FIGURE
10.9

KEYS TO SUCCESS

ADVANCED BACKWARD INSIDE EDGES

Initial Push

1. Strong push to a backward inside edge ___
2. Body box faces to the outside of the circle ___
3. Close thighs ___
4. Rise out of bent skating knee ___

Rotation

5. Turn head to inside of circle ___
6. Bring free foot back ___
7. Drop arms to side of body ___
8. Rotate your body box to inside of circle ___

Transition Push

9. Bring feet together ___
10. Bend both knees ___
11. Push in light switch fashion ___
12. Repeat ___

Comparison of Forward Swingrolls and Advanced Forward Edges

With advanced edges, the goal is to skate perfect circles or semicircles whereas with swingrolls the curve is not perfectly circular. With swingrolls, your body box (as shown by rectangles in Figure 10.10) remains square to the main direction of travel except for the slight distortion of your body box caused by full forward extension of your leg and during the push into the next opposite curve. With advanced forward edges, your body box is square to the direction of travel along the semicircles. In swingrolls, your arms (depicted by straight lines in Figure 10.10) are kept as square to the main direction of travel as possible. With advanced edges, your arms must be "switched" (represented by dots in Figure 10.10) to maintain a circular path and to prepare for the next push.

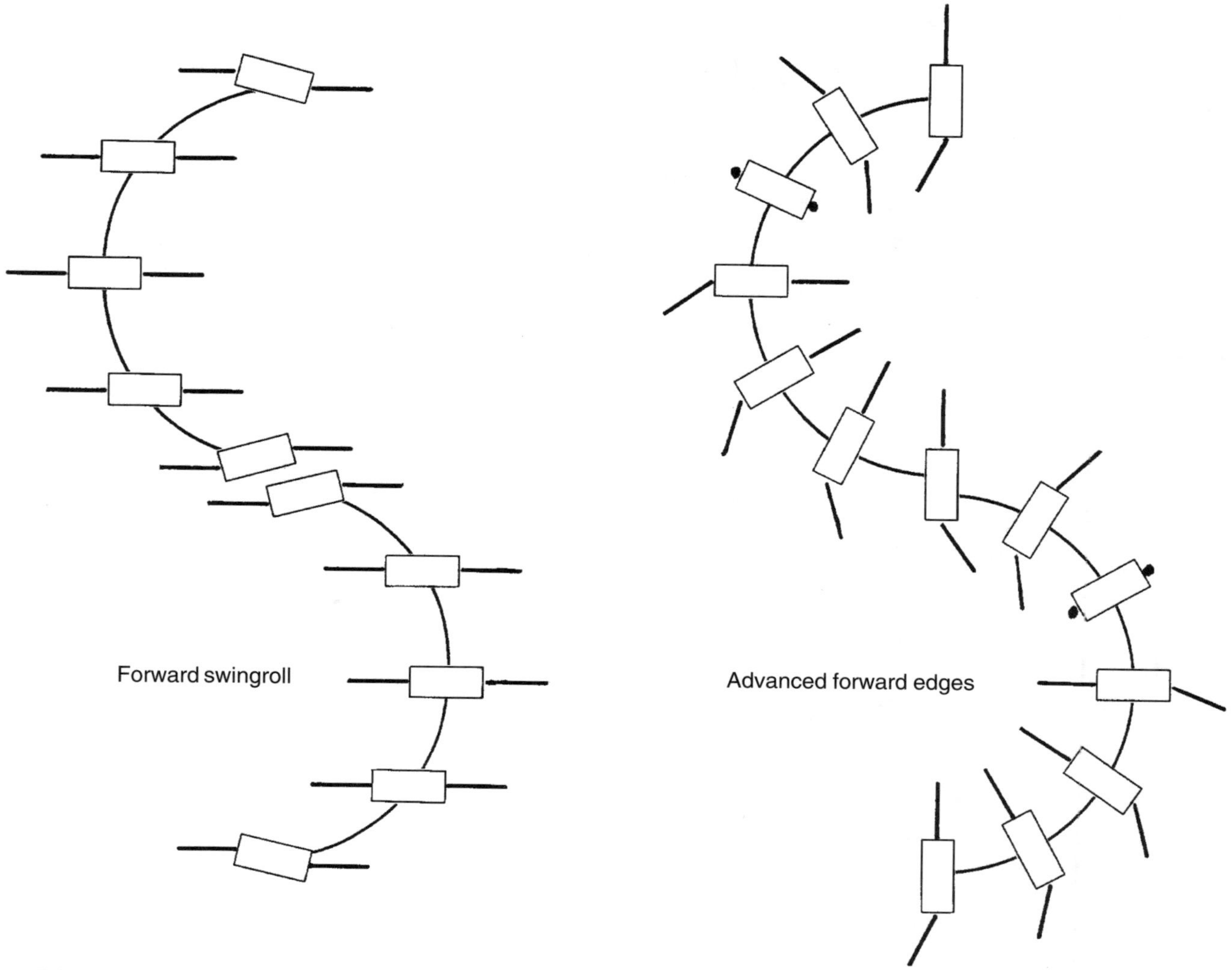

Forward swingroll

Advanced forward edges

Figure 10.10 Comparison of forward swingrolls and advanced edges. With swingrolls, the arms remain outstretched side to side and square to the long skating axis. With advanced edges, the arms are switched in order to rotate the body box, which at times is square to the direction of travel along the circular tracing and at times faces into and at times out of the circle depending on the direction and edge being skated.

SWINGROLLS AND ADVANCED EDGES SUCCESS STOPPERS

The errors for forward and backward swingrolls and advanced edges are amazingly similar, the exception being that on the advanced edges, due to the switching of your arms, an additional possibility to screw up is provided. "Screw up" is an appropriate term because switching your arms incorrectly has the potential to create rotational momentum and twisting of your body in a corkscrew fashion. If your arms are switched at waist or shoulder level instead of being dropped to the sides, an upper body rotation is created that is very hard to control. This lack of control is especially noticeable if you plan to extend your edges into a full circle or into a spiral.

Error	Correction
1. You don't get sufficient speed to travel far enough to do all the moves and maintain your balance.	1. Be sure to bend your knees enough at the push.
2. You push with your body box facing the wrong way or you fail to turn within your arms, which makes you feel like a pretzel.	2. In swingrolls, don't move or switch your arms, as each swingroll should begin with your body box facing the main direction of travel. In advanced edges, switch your arms close to your body.
3. You get too much rotational momentum and your free hip drops because you bring your free leg forward in a wide arc instead of close to your skating foot.	3. Keep the passage of your free leg as close as possible to your skating leg, even to the point of rubbing the insteps of your skates together. Your free leg must be bent to pass close to your skating leg.
4. You rock your upper body backward and forward.	4. Keep your sternum over the toes of your skating foot.
5. You don't seem able to hold onto an edge and fight rotational momentum from the free leg.	5. When your free foot is to the inside or outside of the curve, the skating axis does not pass from your skating foot through the opposite shoulder as it should but tends to pass from your skating foot through your shoulder on the same side. Hold your free foot over the tracing following a push or passage of that leg.
6. Your upper body leans out of the curve.	6. Regardless of the direction your body box is facing, it must always lean into the curve. Your body should lean as a single unit with no secondary bends anywhere.

SWINGROLLS AND ADVANCED EDGES

DRILLS

1. Consecutive Swingrolls

The objective of this drill is to skate a complete "S" shaped figure with each of the four possible types of swingrolls. Your first attempts can be facilitated by taking some initial speed. Do all four swingroll types.

Success Goal = to have an equal amount of speed in each segment of the "S" so that both are equal in size and shape for all four swingrolls ___

✔ **Success Check**
• Free leg passes close to skating leg and extends ___
• Your arms are extended at hip to waist level ___
• Your arms remain in same position from beginning to end ___

To Increase Difficulty
• Once your pushes from a standstill are strong enough to carry you through the first half of the "S," do all four swingrolls from a standstill.

To Decrease Difficulty
• Place second foot on the ice between swingrolls to help reorganize your body box.

2. Swingrolls and Mohawk Combinations

Begin this more demanding drill with four consecutive forward inside swingrolls, go directly into a forward inside mohawk, and finish with four consecutive backward outside swingrolls. Then, start in the other direction so that the opposite side mohawk gets its share of practice too.

Success Goal =
a. to make the forward inside swingrolls and the backward outside swingrolls cover the same amount of ice ___
b. to keep the tempo of the mohawk and swingrolls the same ___

✔ **Success Check**
• Pass your free leg close to skating leg ___
• Turn within your arms ___
• Trace long sweeping curves on the ice ___

To Increase Difficulty
• Try to skate the drill to various tempos of music.

To Decrease Difficulty
• Use two-foot glides after the forward swingrolls in preparation for the mohawk.

3. Half-Circle Advanced Edges

Practice pushes to each of the four edges from a standstill. The first success goal is to complete at least a half-circle with each push. The radius of each semicircle should be at least equal to your height.

Success Goal = the radius of each semicircle must be at least equal to your height ___

Success Check
- Push hard enough to complete the half-circle ___
- Keep body box and head facing as explained ___
- Switch arms and free leg close to body ___

To Increase Difficulty
- Skate identical but opposite interconnected semicircles to either side of the long skating axis.

To Decrease Difficulty
- Put your second foot on the ice for a short two-foot glide in between half-circles to reorganize your body box.

4. Full Circle Advanced Edges

A more advanced set of drills is to complete full circles with each of the four edges possible, beginning with pushes from a standstill.

Success Goal = to generate enough speed with one push per circle to complete a figure-8 ___

Success Check
- Push hard enough to complete the half-circle ___
- Keep body box and head facing as explained ___
- Switch arms and free leg close to body ___

To Increase Difficulty
- Skate a figure-8 with circles of equal diameter.

To Decrease Difficulty
- Add pushes as needed to finish circle.

SWINGROLLS AND ADVANCED EDGES SUCCESS SUMMARY

Swingrolls and advanced edges help you perfect the five basic skating principles. At the same time, they are useful in themselves and are also the foundation for more advanced moves. Because of the nature and difficulty of the skating maneuvers you'll perform at this stage, the five basic principles of ice skating should now be part of your body memory and applied subconsciously. Too much will be happening when you are learning new skills for you to consciously remember the five basic principles. In judging your progress with swingrolls and advanced edges, a trained observer, using the checklists in Figures 10.1 through 10.7 and Figure 10.9, should pay special attention to their similarities and differences.

Rockefeller Center Ice Rink, Manhattan, New York. This is perhaps the most recognized and elegant outdoor ice skating rink in the world. The rink glistens under the golden statue of Prometheus, who ironically brought fire, not ice, to the world.

STEP
11
THREE TURNS: CHANGING DIRECTIONS AND EDGES

In this step we present *three turns*, which are a change in direction from forward to backward or backward to forward on one foot. They are called "three turns" because the tracing on the ice resembles the number 3. Until you can do three turns, it will be difficult to progress to the more challenging skills, such as spins, jumps, and ice dance.

Because of the advanced nature of three turns—more advanced than any other skill taught in this book—your comprehension of the five basic principles of ice skating will be tested. The backward three turns are particularly challenging because all five basic skating principles must be applied for success. Though turning on one ice skate comes very naturally, controlling turns on one skate so that they can be followed by another move is another matter and requires excellent control of your body.

It is likely that three turns have been done voluntarily and involuntarily since the 8th century when Scandinavians first strapped on skates made from walrus teeth and used them for travel in winter. Three turn techniques improved quickly as ice skates and ice skating evolved for racing, games, dance, and figure skating.

Why Are Three Turns Important?

The reason the three turn has been a central part of skating from the beginning is because it occurs very naturally as a result of the slipperiness of ice and the rotational momentum created by speed on a curve. The modern blade with its curvature from front to back and well defined edges makes performing three turns much easier than would have been pos-

sible on the ancient wooden platform skates with flat runners. The three turn is an essential component of modern skating. Once it is mastered, it opens the doors to footwork, jumps, spins, and ice dancing.

How to Execute Forward and Backward Three Turns

By definition, a three turn begins with an entry on one edge and finishes with an exit on the other edge on the same skate. There are four different types of three turns: Forward outside to backward inside, forward inside to backward outside, backward outside to forward inside, and backward inside to forward outside. The point of the three turn is always directed toward the center of the curve. As with all maneuvers that involve a directional change or skating along a curve, your body box is prerotated and that prerotated position is held throughout the turn to minimize rotational momentum. In addition, your arms should be extended over the tracing at about hip to waist level. In the beginning when you first learn how to do a three turn, it is a good idea to start with some speed rather than from a standstill. This helps you maintain your balance and gives you the momentum necessary for the turn. Again, it is important that you review the concepts of your prerotated body box and lean and that you understand your body axis and checking (see Step 8). In the ideal three turn, the shape and size of the entry curve is identical to that of the exit curve. At first you might think that three turns are a full 180 degrees; however, they are actually less because they are skated on a curve and because your body box is already prerotated going into the turn.

Forward Outside Three Turn

Forward outside three turns produce a change of direction from a forward outside edge to a backward inside edge on the same foot (Figure 11.1). When you have reached the desired speed, rotate your body box toward the center of the curve, extend your arms along the tracing with your hands at about waist level and place your free-foot toe at the heel of your skating foot (see Figure 11.1a). Your skating foot will turn almost automatically if you can maintain your body position and visualize the turn as a change of edge from forward outside to backward inside (Figures 11.1b-d). The turn is helped with a slight unweighing of the skate blade produced by a very subtle upward bounce. Except for the fact that you are now on a backward inside edge, nothing has changed (Figure 11.1e). Your body box is still facing the inside of the circle. Your arms are still extended over your tracing. Your head is still looking in the skating direction. Your arms have not switched. You have turned inside your arms. The check on exiting the three turn is achieved simply by maintaining body box rotation (component one of checking), the free side of your body box up (component two of checking) and your arms extended along the tracing (component three of checking). Checking is also aided by keeping your free foot next to your skating foot throughout the turn so that it and your free leg add little rotational momentum (component four of checking).

Forward Inside Three Turn

The forward inside three turn is similar to the forward outside in many ways. The main differences are that it starts on a forward inside edge and ends on a backward outside edge and movement of your free leg can help initiate the turn (see Figure 11.2). Start with a little speed on an inside edge with your body box rotated to face inside the curve (Figures 11.2a and b) (component one of checking). Your free leg should be extended backward with your foot over the tracing. To initiate the turn, bring the lower portion of your free leg from the knee down to the outside of the circle behind your skating foot (Figure 11.2c) (component two of checking). To prevent the rotation of the turn from pulling your free leg too far behind the tracing, which, in turn, will tend to cause your free hip to drop and your body box to be distorted, the big toe of your free foot can be brought in contact with the heel of your skating foot. With your free hip up (component three of checking) and your arms extended over the tracing (component four of checking), you are ready to change from a forward inside edge to a backward outside edge on the same foot (Figures 11.2c and d). A very subtle unweighing with slight bounce just before the turn may help. As you continue on the backward outside edge, your body box rotation tends to lessen and the shoulders and hips become square to the direction of travel (Figure 11.2e).

FIGURE
11.1

KEYS TO SUCCESS

FORWARD OUTSIDE THREE TURN
Prerotation

1. Prerotation and lean of body box ___
2. Arms extended over tracing ___
3. Free-foot toe next to skating foot ___

The Turn

4. Unweigh skate and turn ___

Postturn Check

5. Keep your body box facing to the inside of the curve (component 1 of checking) ___
6. Keep the free side of your body box up (component 2 of checking) ___
7. Keep back arm over tracing (component 3 of checking) ___
8. Keep your free foot next to your skating foot (component 4 of checking) ___

FIGURE
11.2 **KEYS TO SUCCESS**

FORWARD INSIDE THREE TURN

Prerotation

1. Prerotation and lean of your body box ___
2. Arms extended over tracing ___
3. Free leg extended to back ___
4. Free foot over tracing ___

The Turn

5. Bring free foot to back of skating foot to initiate turn ___

Postturn Check

6. Keep your body box facing to the inside of the curve (component 1 of checking) ___
7. Keep the free side of your body box up (component 2 of checking) ___
8. Keep back arm over tracing (component 3 of checking) ___
9. Prevent your free foot from drifting to the inside of the curve (component 4 of checking) ___

Backward Outside Three Turn

Backward three turns differ from their forward counterparts in that your body box must be prerotated to face the outside of the curve being skated rather than to the inside and, therefore, backward three turns require a somewhat more complex preparatory phase. The preparatory outward prerotation of your body box for backward three turns is similar to the sequence in advanced backward edges except your free leg remains in front throughout the entire maneuver (compare Figures 10.7c-i, p. 128, to Figures 11.3a-g). The push, the rise from the skating-knee bend, and change in the direction of your body box with the switch of your arms are all the same. Once your body box is facing the outside of the circle (Figures 11.3f and g), make sure your free hip is still up and your thighs firmly pressed together with your free foot extended and pigeon-toed over your past tracing. For the backward three turn, body box rotation to the outside cannot stop at facing the long axis of travel as in backward outside edges but must be even more severe. This is facilitated by turning your head and looking over your free shoulder and by pressing your free arm back (Figure 11.3g). The actual turn is more like a change of edge from backward outside to forward inside to allow your skating foot to "catch up" with your prerotated body box. To further assist making the turn, unweigh your skating foot with a very slight "bounce." The turn is done inside your arms with your head continuously facing into the direction of travel. Coming out of the three turn, you will find yourself on a solid forward inside edge with your skating arm (the arm on your skating side) stretched over the back tracing and your free arm in front (Figures 11.3h-j). Note how low your free leg is kept and how your thighs do not separate throughout the maneuver.

Backward Inside Three Turn

The backward inside three turn must be entered on a backward inside edge. How you gain the necessary speed to get onto that backward inside edge is immaterial. If the backward inside three is done after a series of backward crossovers, then a rotation of your body box from the inside of the curve to the outside is required (Figures 11.4a-f). For those who can gain sufficient speed with pushes to a back inside edge, you are already in the correct body box and leg position for the back inside three (Figures 11.4e-g; for comparison, review Figures 10.9a-c and j-k, pp. 132-133). As with backward outside three turns, your thighs remain closed, your free foot is pigeon-toed across the tracing, your arms are extended along the tracing, and your head is facing into the direction of travel. To initiate the three turn, a slight backward motion of your skating side arm coupled with a slight bounce of your skating knee will help (Figures 11.4g and h). The turn is a change of edge, inside your arms, from backward inside to forward outside. Your free foot is pointing to where you want to go. On the forward outside exit edge, your skating arm is over your skating foot and your other arm is over the back tracing (Figures 11.4i and j). Your body box remains facing the outside of the circle with your free hip and shoulder slightly higher.

FIGURE
11.3 **KEYS TO SUCCESS**

BACKWARD OUTSIDE THREE TURN
Prerotation

Same as the Keys to Success for Advanced Backward Outside Edges (see Figure 10.7, pp. 128-129) except your free foot remains in front over the tracing.

1. Turn your head to face over free shoulder ___
2. Press your free arm back ___

The Turn

3. Make the turn (a slight bounce helps) ___

Postturn Check

4. Body box remains facing outside of curve ___
5. Head faces in direction of travel ___
6. Thighs remain closed ___
7. Free foot low and over the tracing ___

FIGURE
11.4

KEYS TO SUCCESS

BACKWARD INSIDE THREE TURN

Prerotation

1. Rotate your body box to outside of curve ___
2. Switch arm positions ___
3. Turn head outward to face direction of travel ___
4. Thighs closed ___
5. Free foot pigeon-toed to front over tracing ___

The Turn

6. Turn head to face over free shoulder ___
7. Press free arm back ___
8. Make the turn (a slight bounce helps) ___

Postturn Check

9. Body box remains facing outside of curve ___
10. Head faces in direction of travel ___
11. Thighs remain closed ___
12. Free foot low and over the tracing ___

THREE TURNS SUCCESS STOPPERS

The mere performance of a three turn does not necessarily ensure success because improper placement of your body box during the exit may not allow you to proceed to your next desired move or may even cause you to lose your balance. Errors in the mechanics manifest themselves mainly in the postturn checking phase. There, the loss of control is most obvious. If at the approach, something feels out of control, it may be best to abandon that particular try since the chances of success are severely diminished.

Error	Correction
Forward Three Turns	
1. You experience difficulties controlling the backward edge after the three turn (a whipping effect from the free leg).	1. Your free leg is too far from your skating foot during the turn. Keep your free foot and leg close to your skating foot.
2. You are compelled to put your free foot on the ice because of loss of balance (barn door effect).	2. When the free hip is down, too much body mass is left on one side of that axis of rotation. Distribute your body weight so it is balanced around the axis of rotation, like a revolving door.
3. Your body box does not face the inside of the curve.	3. If you're finding it hard to rotate your hips equally with your shoulders, try turning your buttocks to face the outside of the curve.
4. You lean your body box out of the curve.	4. Remember the medallion principle has two components: Prerotation of your body box and lean of your body box to the inside of the curve.
5. You switch arms.	5. Do all turns within the arms (review Step 8, p. 87). Your arms remain outstretched over the tracing being skated.
6. The skate blade skids during the three turn.	6. The skid is most often caused by the skating foot being too upright and not enough on an edge during the entry curve.

Error	Correction
Backward Three Turns	
1. You displace the skating axis at the time of body box rotation.	1. Keep the free side of your body box tilted up.
2. You rotate your body box by leaning forward and out of the curve when entering the three turn.	2. Bend your skating knee and lift your free hip slightly so that your body weight is squarely over the entry edge.
3. You lose control during the turn and feel like you might fall backward.	3. You lean backward during the change of edge at the time of the turn. Keep your thighs pressed together, your free leg low, and tighten your abdominal muscles.
4. You separate your thighs, making your skating foot feel stuck at the turn.	4. Separating the thighs has a tendency to cause your free hip to drop too low. This in turn takes your weight off the entry edge and can make you change your edge before the turn or even make it impossible to turn at all.
5. You switch arms during the three turn.	5. Keep your arms still and rotate within them (Principle #5).
6. You look back after the three turn.	6. Your body weight will tend to fall backward and out of the circle on the exit. Keep your head facing in the skating direction.

THREE TURNS

DRILLS

1. Individual Three Turns

The forward outside and inside three turns are used so frequently in ice skating that particular attention must be paid to practicing them in both directions until they are committed to muscle memory. The backward three turns are advanced maneuvers and are used in more specialized situations. However, just because forward three turns are used more often than backward do not let that keep you from practicing the backward three turns to both sides.

Because most people are right handed and since the main direction of travel on most rinks is counterclockwise, a preference for body box rotation and lean in that direction develops early with forward crossovers. The same rotation and lean of the body box are needed for the left forward outside and right forward inside three turns, which is probably why these seem easier to learn at first. Begin by practicing the forward outside three turns and then the forward inside three turns to both sides.

For the same reasons, there are also preferences for backward three turns with most skaters finding the right back outside three and the left back inside three easier. However, you should practice all of the back three turns.

Success Goal =

a. to complete all four types of three turns ___
b. to skate symmetrical threes with the exit tracing the same length and same radius curve as the entry for all four types of three turns ___
c. to do all four types of three turns smoothly within your arms and hold the exit edge for at least the same distance as your height ___

Success Check

• Prerotate your body box going into the turn ___
• Hold your prerotated position throughout the turn ___
• Enter on one edge and exit on the other edge on the same skate ___
• Direct the point of the three turn toward the center of the curve ___
• Extend arms over the tracing of the curve ___

To Increase Difficulty

• Exit any of the three turns with enough control to continue gliding on that edge as long as you please or proceed to the next desired move.

To Decrease Difficulty

• Use a preparatory push to gain momentum for the turn and shorten the distance traveled on the exit edge.

2. Combinations With Three Turns

The following are a few of many possible ways in which three turns can be combined with other moves you have learned. The main value of combining multiple different maneuvers is it requires that you have committed each of the skills to memory so that you can focus on the sequence and style of the skills rather than on the mechanics of the individual skill.

Sample combinations follow:

a. Begin with a forward outside three turn, then step to a backward outside edge on the other foot, step forward to an outside edge, then do a forward inside three turn on your other foot and repeat. Do this to both sides.

b. Begin with a forward inside three turn, step onto a backward inside edge, and do a backward inside three turn. Do to both sides.

c. Begin with a forward outside three turn, step on a backward outside edge, and do a backward outside three turn. Do to both sides.

d. Start with a backward crossover, do a backward outside three turn, then do a forward inside mohawk and repeat. Do to both sides.

Success Goal = to do each component of the four sample combinations with the same tempo and speed ___

Success Check
- Use proper technique (review Figures 11.1 through 11.4, as necessary) ___

To Increase Difficulty
- Add music.
- Add your own style to these combinations.
- Create your own mini-routines including as many skills as possible to both sides such as forward and backward crossovers, swingrolls, advanced edges, mohawks, three turns, and so forth.

To Decrease Difficulty
- Shorten the length of any particular combination.
- Use steps in between to regain speed.

THREE TURNS SUCCESS SUMMARY

Three turns must incorporate four of the five basic principles of ice skating to be done correctly. Your body weight must remain centered over your skating foot (weight over skating foot principle). Your body box (hips and shoulders) must be aligned throughout the turn (body box principle). Your body box must be prerotated and lean into the curve (the medallion principle). The degree of lean must remain constant on the entry and exit from the turn. Finally, because of prerotation of your body box with the arms extended over the tracing, only your skating foot catches up with the rest of your body (turn within your arms principle). The paramount "key to success" is to develop the confidence to do all of the above on the edge of the ice skate blade, not on the flat of the blade.

The main purpose of prerotation of your body box and the turn within your arms principles is to minimize the effort required to stop the rotational momentum of large body parts during turns.

You may hear many skating instructors teaching students to rotate their shoulders and arms strongly while keeping their hips nonrotated to develop a diagonal tension in the body box. They argue that this tension creates the force to complete the three turn. The problem with this alternative method is that it causes the hips to rotate rapidly during the turn. Because of the mass of the hips, a rotational momentum is created that is very difficult to control without a vigorous counter-checking. This is probably why these same teachers are continually yelling, "Check!"

A trained observer should pay attention to whether or not the basic ice skating principles are being followed and that the specifics for each three turn are being executed according to the checklists in Figures 11.1 through 11.4.

STYLE AND EFFICIENCY: RATING YOUR SKATING PROGRESS

Needless to say, people do not ice skate to be efficient. Virtually every skater skates because skating is fun and challenging. Whether someone skates for speed, for the challenge of jumps, for the roughness of hockey, or for the gracefulness and romance of dance, sooner or later his or her skating style emerges. The fullest expression of style, as with any complex endeavor, requires a solid understanding of the basic principles involved. Only when these principles are committed to muscle memory will you have the ability to mold and bend them in your own way. How do you commit the basic principles to muscle memory? Through practice.

Style: The Consequence and Benefit of Efficient Skating

Watching a hockey game and comparing it with figure skating, or watching ice dancing and comparing it to freestyle, you may think that the skaters from these different disciplines have not much more in common than the ice they skate on and the skates on their feet. However, the basic skating techniques as described in this book are very much alike for each of the different kinds of skating. The ability to move forward and backward with efficiency, to stop from every speed and position, and to turn in any direction are fundamental to ice skating, no matter which skating sport you choose to pursue.

Hockey skaters develop a unique style mainly because of their desire to accurately hit and direct the puck with the stick and score goals. Their need to be fast and stable (and at times aggressive and defensive) obviously has a great deal of influence on their skating style. Even at a public skating session, the style of those who have played hockey is distinctive with its rapid bursts of speed, quick stops, and short aggressive stroking. In contrast, ice dancers, although restricted by rules and regulations of dance patterns, have the benefit of music and a partner. Their style, influenced by ballroom dance and artistic expression, makes their skating distinctive. Speed skaters, in their skin-tight speed suits, bent over with their chests parallel to the ice and gliding at top speed with long, powerful strokes in a continuously counterclockwise world, have a style that anyone can recognize. Last are the figure and freestyle skaters who combine the most rigorous and challenging athleticism with varying degrees of artistry.

As you watch professional and competitive skaters, you may find yourself envious of the ease with which they perform both simple and complex feats on thin ice skate blades. Always remember, like you, they had to start at the beginning. Those who reach the top often have the benefit of talent teamed with outstanding ice skating instructors; however, they also had the determination to succeed, to accept failure, to work through injuries, and to persist in their pursuit of their goals.

Effective Practice Procedures

If the style and level of skating expertise you see on TV, at shows, or at the hockey arena doesn't seem to have many similarities with what you're working on, try to follow the instructions in this book, and don't forget that this is just the beginning. Once you gain confidence in doing the basic moves, you'll automatically develop your own unique style. Where before it took a lot of thinking just to do a simple step, that step now comes easily. This is called "muscle memory." Early on you'll have all of the information in your head, but your body won't seem to be willing to follow the instructions. On average, people must be exposed to information about seven times before their brain and muscles absorb it. Rarely will the body actually do what the brain commands. Often you'll have so much information about what to do and what not to do that a state of "analysis paralysis" sets in. In this case, it is best to make a choice of what is most useful and important. At other times, skating maneuvers will come automatically. Leave these alone. Concentrate only on what is wrong, and fix it. Start with four or five things that prevent you from progressing with a maneuver and list them to be practiced in chronological order. Eventually, several items on your list will become easier to perform and you'll need to concentrate less on them. You can then replace them with more difficult goals to practice.

Rating Your Ice Skating Progress

Ice skating can provide enjoyable exercise no matter what your skill level, but you'll have more fun as your skills improve. Check your progress with the basic ice skating principles by answering *yes* or *no* to the following questions about your skating skills.

Basic Ice Skating Principles

1. While skating forward or backward in a straight line, do you keep your head up and your sternum over the toes of your skating foot? ___
2. Do you keep your hands at the periphery of your vision? ___
3. Do you keep your shoulders and hips aligned? ___
4. When stroking or performing other maneuvers requiring a weight transfer from one foot to the other, can you do it without placing both feet on the ice at the same time? ___
5. When thrusting to gain speed with the light switch method, do you push with the inside edge of the blade and not the toepick? ___
6. When skating on a curve, do you rotate both your shoulders and hips (body box) equally and as a single unit into or out of the curve as required? ___
7. When your body box is rotated toward the inside of a curve being skated, do you also lean your body box into the curve so that your sternum is over a point inside the tracing? ___
8. When your body box is rotated to the outside of the curve being skated such as with backward three turns, is your sternum kept over your skating toes? ___

9. When changing direction from forward to backward or backward to forward, do you prerotate your body box and keep it rotated throughout the turn? ___

10. When skating on one blade on an outside edge, do you keep the free hip up? ___

11. When skating on a single blade on an inside edge, do you keep your free hip level with the skating hip? ___

12. Related to the previous two questions, when skating on one blade, does a vertical line (the skating axis) pass from your skating foot through your opposite shoulder? ___

13. Do you keep your weight-supporting knee bent? ___

14. Do you keep your head facing into the direction of travel particularly with backward crossovers and during three turns and mohawks? ___

Using Edges

1. For stroking, crossovers, three turns, mohawks, and swingrolls, are you skating on the edge of the blade? ___

2. Are you cheating by skating on the flat of the blade? ___

3. Is your tracing a single line created by a single edge cutting through the ice? Or is it a double line caused by skating on the flat of the blade? ___

Skating Safely

1. Are your stopping skills as good as your skating skills? ___

2. Have you learned how to skate safely? ___

3. Is your equipment appropriate? ___

4. Do you leave enough room on the ice to complete your maneuvers and respect the space of others skating around you? ___

5. Do you check ice conditions before beginning to skate? ___

The principles of ice skating and the ice skating skills presented in this book will give you the freedom to do whatever you want on the ice. Floating across a shining field of ice with your arms stretched out and the wind rushing at your face and through your hair gives an incomparable feeling. To us, it is the closest thing to flying.

GLOSSARY

body axis—Same as skating axis.

body box—The part of the body within a rectangle formed by the corners of the hips and shoulders.

crossover—A maneuver to gain speed on a curve or circle where the feet are crossed and uncrossed with pushes.

edges, skating—Terms used by skaters that refer to gliding half- or full circles on a continuous edge on one foot forward or backward.

free foot—Foot held above the ice in contrast to the skating foot.

free side—The shoulder, arm, hip, and leg on the free-foot side of the body.

hockey glide—A curved glide on two feet in an in-line position with the foot in the front on an outside edge and the foot in the back on an inside edge.

hockey stop—A stop with both feet turned perpendicular to the skating direction for a controlled skid with back foot on an outside edge and front foot on an inside edge.

inside edge—The bottom portion of the blade to the inside of your leg.

long axis—Actual or imaginary straight line over which a pattern of curves, half-circles, or zigzags are skated.

mohawk—Change of foot on a curve from forward to backward or backward to forward on edges of the same character.

outside edge—The bottom portion of the blade to the outside of your leg.

rotational axis—It is the same as the skating or body axis but used in the context of maneuvers in which body rotation occurs.

skateboard pushes—Repetitive pushes on a circle with the foot on the outside of the curve doing the pushing and the other foot gliding on an outside edge.

skating axis—An imaginary vertical line from the skating foot through the body around which the body weight should be equally distributed.

skating foot—Foot on which the skater is gliding or standing in contrast to the free foot, which is the foot held off the ice.

skating posture—The carriage of the body with the sternum over the toes and the abdomen tucked in.

skating side—Shoulder, arm, hip, and leg on the same side as the skating foot.

slalom—Consecutive parallel curves produced by skating forward on two feet to both sides of the main line of travel.

snowplow stop—A stop with one foot continuing straight in the skating direction and the stopping foot turned at a 45-degree angle to produce a skid. For the forward snowplow stop, the skidding foot is turned in (pigeon-toed). For the backward snowplow stop, the skidding foot is turned out.

stopping foot—The foot placed at an angle to the skating direction to produce a skid.

stroking—Consecutive pushes from one foot to the other on either inside or outside edges, forward or backward.

swingroll—One-foot curve on an inside or outside edge where the free foot is swung from full extension in the pushing direction to full extension in the skating direction.

swizzles—Mirror image wavy lines produced by skating on inside edges on both feet.

T-stop—Stop with the feet in a T-position and with the front foot gliding forward and back stopping foot placed perpendicular to the skating direction with instep at heel of gliding foot.

three turn—Rotation on one foot from forward to backward or backward to forward with a change of edge.

toepick—The part of the blade in the front with a saw-like shape which is used mainly for jumps.

two-foot turns—A change of direction from forward to backward with feet in an in-line position.

wiggles—The equivalent of a forward slalom, consisting of skating backward on two feet with the skate blades parallel.

ABOUT THE AUTHORS

Jerry Watson Photography

Murry Kalish Photography

Karin Künzle-Watson, one of the world's most prominent ice skating instructors, began her skating career at the age of 6. A former champion at the novice and junior levels, Karin earned seven Swiss national senior titles during her career. She has also placed in many international competitions, including seven European championships, five World championships, and one Olympic appearance. She is one of the few people in the world to have passed Gold Tests (qualifying tests for competition at the highest levels) in all areas of skating—singles, pairs, and dance.

Karin is also an accomplished instructor, having been School Director and Head Professional at the Skating School of St. Gervais and Megève (France) and School Director of the Skating School of San Mateo (U.S.). She presently travels internationally to attend her students' competitions, to teach, and to conduct skating and coaching seminars. Her students consistently rank highly in national and international competitions.

Stephen J. DeArmond, MD, PhD, began ice skating at the age of 47 because he wanted a high-energy, low-impact exercise that was enjoyable enough to do several times weekly. Karin Künzle-Watson's approach to basics helped him to become an accomplished recreational skater. Stephen helped Karin organize her lessons into five basic principles—the foundation of this book—and directed the illustrations and photography. Stephen is a Professor of Neuropathology and Neurology at the University of California, San Francisco, with special research interests in the effects of aging on the central nervous system and skeletal muscle. In this book, DeArmond shares insights based on the health benefits of ice skating, especially to improve both strength and coordination, as well as information on the causes and prevention of injuries.

Stephen is the author and illustrator of *Structure of the Human Brain*, a best-selling textbook of neuroanatomy.

Technique and training on and off the ice

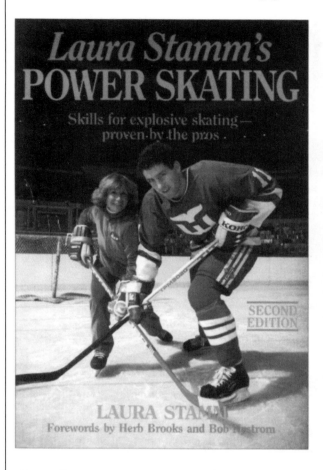

Laura Stamm

Forewords by Herb Brooks and Bob Nystrom
1989 • Paper • 256 pp • Item PSTA0331
ISBN 0-88011-331-6 • $18.95 ($27.95 Canadian)

"By applying the principles outlined in this text a dramatic improvement can rapidly occur. The book offers so many precise pointers, that you almost have to take it with you onto the ice to remember all of the details."
 Lloyd Nesbitt, DPM
 Book Review Editor
 Canadian Podiatric Sports Medicine Academy

"Laura's success at helping players improve their speed, agility, and mobility is unquestionable. She is a great coach."
 Rogatien Vachon
 President, Los Angeles Kings

Don MacAdam, MPE, and Gail Reynolds, MA
1988 • Paper • 152 pp • Item PMAC0314
ISBN 0-88011-314-6 • $14.95 ($20.95 Canadian)

Hockey Fitness is a complete conditioning resource that will help you improve strength, endurance, flexibility, quickness, speed, and recovery. You'll also learn how to set training objectives and optimize training effects using the principles of overload and adaptation, reversibility, and specificity.

MacAdam and Reynolds will tell you how to minimize negative influences on conditioning through proper nutrition and eating habits, efficient training levels, adaptation to hot environments, illness and injury prevention and care, stress management, and positive attitude.

Human Kinetics
The Premier Publisher for Sports & Fitness
2335

To place an order: U.S. customers call **TOLL-FREE**
1-800-747-4457; customers outside of U.S. use the appropriate telephone number/address shown in the front of this book.

Other books in the
Steps to Success Activity Series

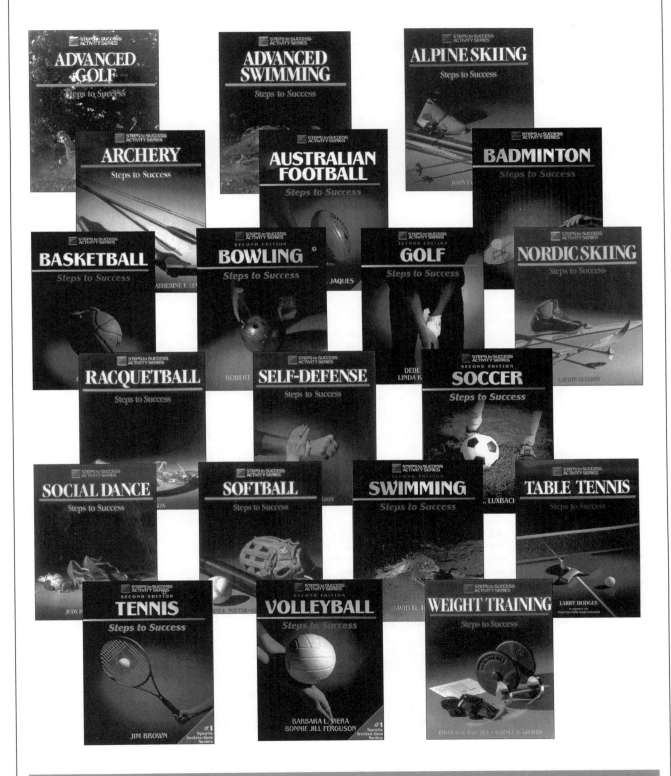